# Preaching Funerals in the Black Church

## Bringing Perspective to Pain

PETER M. WHERRY

Foreword by Charles G. Adams
Preface by Luke A. Powery

JUDSON PRESS
PUBLISHERS SINCE 1824
VALLEY FORGE, PA

**Preaching Funerals in the Black Church: Bringing Perspective to Pain**



Interior design by Crystal Devine.
Cover design by Wendy Ronga, Hampton Design Group.
Cover art is titled "Funeral Procession" by Ellis Wilson. Used by permission.

Library of Congress Cataloging-in-Publication data

Wherry, Peter M.
Preaching funerals in the Black church : bring perspective to pain / Peter M. Wherry ; foreword by Charles Adams. -- First edition
pages cm
ISBN 978-0-8170-1735-4 (pbk. : alk. paper) 1. African American preaching. 2. Death--Religious aspects--Christianity. 3. Funeral sermons. I. Title.
BV4222.W48 2013
251'.1--dc23

2013004148

Printed in the U.S.A.
First Edition, 2013.

# Contents

# Foreword

DR. PETER M. WHERRY has done a great service to those who are called upon to preach funerals. This book will be widely read by pastors everywhere who diligently study and fervently pray to preach good news in bad times. Sudden, unexpected, and shocking deaths can be so shattering that the surviving child, the spouse left behind, the friend deserted find it more than they can do to recover. What do you say when you don't know what to say? Dr. Wherry offers dependence on God and the discipline to read the Bible with exegetical eyes. His wisdom will open up such insights and declarations of faith that the miracle of recovery from a broken heart will occur as the listener gleans treasures of truth that lighten the burden of trying tribulations.

These preaching instructions will doubtlessly improve the art and science of preaching when there is little time to prepare a "customized" message for a grieving family and shattered community. It is the most difficult thing in the world to preach a new sermon to the same family that just witnessed your last best funeral sermon. Dr. Wherry has given us enough methods and examples of great funeral sermons that we will be aided profoundly to see, to sense, and to say something new.

If we can only teach our grieving families to avoid the long funeral that is overburdened with endless repetitions and remarks that leave little room for the attentive reception of the eulogy. Scattered remarks are the bane and burden of all occasions. The audience will little note nor long remember the spate of spontaneous, off-the-cuff, stream of consciousness jibberings of those who demand to make remarks at the funeral. Our greatest task will be to teach our congregations to rule out all remarks so that the place and power and persuasion of preaching may take its place in the heart, mind, and soul of those who are walking through the valley of the shadow of death.

This great book will find a most glorious welcome in all colleges and seminaries that seek to prepare ministers and lay leaders for public service and private witness. We thank the Reverend Dr. Peter M. Wherry for this demonstration of textual analysis, philosophical depth, theological clarification, exegetical diligence, and powerful anointing of the Holy Spirit. If we follow the author's suggestions and examples, "the glory of the Lord shall be revealed and all flesh shall see it together, for the mouth of the Lord has spoken it" (Isaiah 40:5).

**Charles G. Adams**
*Pastor, Hartford Memorial Baptist Church*
*Detroit, Michigan*

# Preface

PETER M. WHERRY IS A pastor-preacher. Not all preachers are good pastors and not all pastors can preach. These two callings are not necessarily synonymous. However, Rev. Wherry does both effectively and faithfully and has done so for many years. He's in touch with the joys and sorrows of humanity on a daily basis. He writes from the trenches of the Christian ministry—on the ground with the faithful people of God in congregational life. A part of these ministerial trenches is dealing with death, something we all must face and something that is all too familiar in many urban African American communities. What Rev. Wherry helps pastor-preachers do, however, is to face death with faith and courage, rather than fear.

This book is a gutsy grappling with the call to preach at funerals, particularly in the black church (though this work clearly has relevance for any church situation). When faced with death, Rev. Wherry does not shrink back in a fetal position of fear, but he writes as one with a faith that knows the God whose love is stronger than death in Jesus Christ. He presents this homiletical guide for funeral preaching in order to "bring perspective to pain."

Pain is an eternal part of the human condition on earth; thus, in practical and theological ways, Rev. Wherry helps preachers learn how to proclaim hope and minister in the midst of pain. He keeps it real as he shares stories of those with whom he has ministered and demonstrates as a pastor how preaching at funerals is never disconnected from the social location of a family. Preaching is never acontextual. It is something that happens somewhere.

The structure of this book reveals this as a literary journey that begins in the concrete experience of pastoral care. From there, the book travels to preaching philosophy and preaching practice, closing with exemplary funeral sermons and eulogies. In the classroom of Wherry, we are taught that funeral preaching "begins before the service starts." This alone should tell the reader that this book is written by a homiletical sage. The Holy Ghost water from this pastor-preacher extraordinaire is refreshing. There is wisdom in this well, and all who are thirsty for more knowledge and understanding about preaching at funerals should drink from it.

**Luke A. Powery, MDiv, ThD**
*Dean of Duke Chapel*
*Associate Professor of the Practice of Homiletics*
*Duke Divinity School*

# Acknowledgments

THIS BOOK IS DEDICATED to the countless families and their departed loved ones who have allowed me to share with them in the precious journey from death to life. It is a rare privilege to have walked with so many through the always difficult and often uplifting experience of a loved one who transitions to the other side.

I especially want to thank the congregations which have afforded me this privilege. I love each of these churches in a particular way. The ideas in this book have all been forged in the crucible of ministry in these great and unique churches. Many thanks to the Pleasant Plain Baptist Church of Drewryville, Virginia. The late Edward Walden, a deacon, guided me as a new pastor through my first encounters with death within a congregation and gave me both wise advice and character-building respect. These things gave me the courage to minister to others with confidence. The late Robert Carey, a faithful deacon and beloved friend, has been a particular inspiration. Long talks in the study, at his home, and cherished conferences at Dairy Queen cemented in me the determination always to seek and value the wisdom of the collective church.

Many thanks as well to the Fountain Baptist Church of Richmond, Virginia. I am particularly grateful to George Branch Jr. and George Greene Sr. George Branch's faithful support as a deacon helped me to navigate the increasingly complex issues of life and death in an urban context. I literally owe my life to this man who helped me learn to minister God's grace to people in need even as forces of darkness press in. I thank God for his friendship and that of his precious wife, Margaret. George Greene is a deacon who demonstrated the powerful message of perseverance through changing seasons by the tenacity with which he has stood on his post.

My thanks also go out to the congregation of the historic Queen Street Baptist Church of Norfolk, Virginia. For sixteen years of ministry in Norfolk, Queen Street afforded me the opportunity to see aspects of ministry in times of death which were complex and demanding such that I am a better pastor, scholar, and preacher than I ever otherwise could have been. I am thankful for the late Willie C. Jones, an archetypal deacon from the old school, who never missed an assignment and who showed me the importance of attention to detail when handling the hearts of others. I am eternally grateful to Linfred Moore Sr., a tremendous deacon, trusted and beloved friend, and a decorated Marine who brought a sense of duty, loyalty, and self-sacrifice to the work of servant leadership which is my guidebook to this day.

My gratitude extends, in addition, to the marvelous people of the Mayfield Memorial Missionary Baptist Church of Charlotte, North Carolina. Mayfield provides for me now a fertile field of service and labor, and they afford the profound privilege of making full proof of my ministry. I am grateful and excited to be pastor of a church with such overwhelming potential. Mayfield's astute and discerning listeners have helped me to sharpen my axe, and their eager, obedient "followship" has reinvigorated my confidence that the local church can be what God will use to redeem the world.

This book could not have been completed without the expert and focused efforts of friends who reviewed the manuscript or offered sage advice at various stages beginning with Dr. Dwayne A. Walker, whose preaching during a funeral I attended in his church, Little Rock, A.M.E.Z. in Charlotte, North Carolina, inspired the phrase, "Bringing Perspective to Pain." I am also profoundly grateful to: Dr. Brad Braxton, Dr. Kirk Byron Jones, Dr. Gregory K. Moss, Dr. Robert G. Murray, Dr. Micah L. McCreary and Pastor Jacqueline M. Madison-McCreary, Dr. Mary H. Young, and Dr. Toney L. McNair Jr. Thanks also go to Dr. Wyatt Tee Walker, who encouraged and counseled me early in my journey as a writer; to Dr. Roland J. Hill, who mentored me and caused Wanda and me to write our first book; to Mayfield's church administrator, Rev. Alvis L. Yates; and to others who along the way have mentored and taught me unselfishly. Thanks as well to Jim Carlson, my very able and helpful research assistant, without whose help I never would have finished this work. Thank you, Dr. Octavia Baker, for your early readings of the manuscript and for introducing me to Jim.

I am thankful to and for the beautiful and brilliant Dr. Wanda Hunter Wherry, my wife of thirty-three years. Wanda, you are the daily evidence of God's love for me. Finally, I thank God for the two phenomenal adults who are our children, Justin and Bethany, and for Wanda's mom, Granny "Tim." Without all of you, my journey would indeed be in and not through the valley of the shadow of death. I love you.

# Introduction

## Where's Mrs. Binkley?

I ARRIVED AT THE CHURCH an hour early to do what in those days was my usual preparation before a funeral. I made certain the temperature was comfortable in the church, I inspected my robe to ensure it was not wrinkled, I walked about the sanctuary and fellowship areas to be sure they were in order, and then I went back to my study to look over the eulogy I had prepared for Mrs. Marilyn Binkley,[1] a long-time and faithful member of the church.

I was pleased that what I had prepared captured the essence of the life of this kind and beloved member, so when the time came for the funeral cortege to arrive, I made my way to the narthex to meet them. I saw that the procession was fairly long and the lead car pulled up to the corner, but I did notice that there seemed to be no hearse. I assumed it had pulled around the corner to accommodate the long procession behind it.

When the mortician and the family entered the narthex, there were no pallbearers and there was no coffin. I turned and from behind my hand asked the mortician, *sotto voce*, "Where's Mrs. Binkley?" He jutted out his arms matter-of-factly and rather loudly responded, "Here she is," handing me a square marble box which contained the cremains of Mrs. Marilyn Binkley.

I had met with the family prior to the service, I had planned everything as completely as I could, but there was one detail I never ascertained: that their mother, Mrs. Binkley, would be cremated prior to the service. Although the number of cremations is on the rise, among African Americans cremations are still relatively rare, and in those days, nearly thirty years ago, cremation was almost unheard of. As pastor, I was forced impromptu to rethink all the plans which had been made by me and by the church. I asked one of the deaconesses to prepare a small offering table by retrieving some of the white linens used for communion and draping it. I asked the church clerk to locate the 8x10 photograph of Mrs. Binkley we had used for the front of the funeral program, and we set it up as artistically as possible on the table alongside the urn.

Most importantly, I as pastor had to quickly rethink the entire approach I would take to this service and to preaching the eulogy of this saintly woman. Some members of the family were upset that because of financial constraints, cremation had become a last resort. Prior to entering the sanctuary, they tearfully and simply betrayed what unbeknownst to them were deep theological questions about the eschatological implications of this move. For the first time, all of my personal preparation was useless, and I found myself yearning somewhat frantically for a resource to help me navigate these uncertain waters. After much reflection on hundreds of experiences with dying, death, and funerals, I have concluded that the time has come to offer some of the gleanings from those experiences to others.

My prayer is that this book will add value to the ministries of pastors and preachers from all traditions, cultures, and faith perspectives, so that they can be better prepared than I was that fateful day many years ago. The title "pastor" is frequently used in this book, merely because in most instances in churches it is the pastor who does the preaching at funerals. This is not to suggest that the concepts and ideas in this volume do not apply to assistant and associate ministers; they most assuredly do. It is understood and acknowledged that there are times when assistants or associates conduct funerals as well.

What is proposed here is a new approach to preaching funerals which will be pastoral, holistic, and healing. I seek to offer in this book a new kind of homiletics text which purports not only to uncover the mechanics and methodology of preaching but also to propose a reimaging of the content of preaching during a time of death. I hope to assist preachers in approaching the task of funeral preaching as an incarnational engagement between grieving persons and the risen Christ. This book is designed to be a new kind of homiletics text: a guidebook for preaching which seeks to provide both tools and practical application of those tools.

If used properly, this volume can be useful for preaching of any kind, not simply for funerals, because it deals with preaching in its essence—a biblical message which seeks to move people toward transformation. I hope that this work will be useful for students in Bible colleges and seminaries and for busy pastors who need an approachable yet scholarly resource for priming the pump of preaching which at times runs dry. I hope that pastors will also use this book as a resource for teaching the associate ministers in their charge. As I write this book, I am myself a busy pastor, and I only wish someone had written this volume many years ago for me.

I offer these pages so that the primordial task of the preacher can be discharged with excellence, that God's herald during times of death in the church will be found bringing perspective to pain, and consequently, preaching funerals with power.

---

**NOTES**

1. Unless otherwise indicated, names of the deceased and their families have been changed to preserve confidentiality.

▪ PART ONE ▪

# Preparing Funeral Sermons

• CHAPTER 1 •

# Funeral Preaching Begins before the Service Starts

## It's What's Up Front That Counts

*If God is with us, it means we are not alone. It means we are not alone in our dark dungeons of despair. It means we are not alone in the moments when we feel most lonely and isolated. It means that in the midst of our remote island prisons of sin we are not in solitary confinement. We have a cellmate and he is God incarnate.*[1]

I ONCE HAD A VOICE TEACHER, the renowned baritone Eugene Bayless at Indiana University in Bloomington, who repeatedly stressed to me during lessons, "It's what's up front that counts." I had to sing for many years before I really understood what he meant by that remark, but in summary he meant that vocal production must involve lifting the upper lip, flaring the nostrils "like a colt," showing the teeth, relaxing and dropping the lower jaw—up-front work. Without this, he wanted me to know, the sound will not be correct. In vocal production, this sequence of events enables the air to go up into the head and bounce off the vocal resonators, causing the sound produced to be able to spin and be focused, richer and giving the sense of being louder. Although it can be argued that what happens with the jaw, teeth, and upper lip are the result rather than the beginning, these actions are what is most visible to the people who are beneficiaries of the art of singing. "Peter," Mr. Bayless said, "it's what's up front that counts."

Many years later I understand that without this up-front work (that is, the preparation behind what people see and hear), all the effort of singing will be wasted and useless. What looks like an effortless, spontaneous song is really the result of a lot of up-front work. This same maxim is true when preparing to preach funerals in the church. The up-front work, the vital and indispensible work of presentation which is the point of contact with hearers, is at the same time done before standing behind the sacred desk. This up-front work is done before the preacher even sits down to write the eulogy or the funeral sermon. This understanding is critical to successfully engaging the preaching task.

## Contact Is Crucial

The event of a death in a family will always bring out the best in people, and it will always bring out the worst in people. This is why it is vitally important for the preacher to engage the family personally at some level. Nowadays, we are in the era of the megaministry in which the preacher of the eulogy is rarely the one who makes initial contact, or even any contact, with the family, but this one step is more crucial to preaching than text selection, exegesis, or even delivery of the message. James Forbes, in a lecture on homiletics at the Hampton Ministers' Conference many years ago, argued that a preacher's first task is not to exegete the text but to exegete the audience.[2] Contact with a family prior to the funeral is the prime opportunity to do human exegesis. In this process of exegesis, the preacher has the opportunity to discern the dynamics at work in a family and to glean valuable insights into the life of the deceased. The preacher also can gauge whether a family is encountering the best or the worst dynamics of the process of death and dying. These insights will prove invaluable as the preacher enjoins the tasks of text selection, exegesis, and delivery.

The social worker in me has taught me the importance of evaluating carefully the environment in which a family lives. Poverty need not involve a negative experience with death, but it may give some insight into whether a family is struggling with the financial aspects of death. It may also cause the preacher to be alert to tensions within the family surrounding finances. It should be said, however, that tension over funeral finances is an equal opportunity divider of families. Oftentimes, families of means have even more divisive struggles over finances, because some member of the family senses or perhaps knows that substantial sums of money or other assets may be at stake.

Sign the guestbook if one is provided in the home. Signing the guestbook affords the opportunity to see how many others have also signed it. The number of people listed in the guestbook indicates to some extent the level of regard for the deceased or for the family. This is also a valuable insight to keep in mind when preparing for the preaching task. A person well thought-of carries different exegetical implications than someone or some family who appears fairly isolated in such a time of need.

Make a mental note of the sights and sounds inside the home. Is the place dark, or are plenty of lights turned on? If the visit occurs during daylight hours, are the blinds or curtains open? If the place is dark, it is likely that the emotional mood or psychological mindset of the family is also dark. A dark home may also send a message about the physical state of the people inside. The stress and distress of grief may cause a flare-up of chronic conditions such as migraine headaches, shortness of breath, or heart palpitations.

Be sure to remove your overcoat if you are wearing one, and allow it to be hung up if this is offered. The family must not sense that you are in a hurry, even if you are. Put your keys away. Jangling keys are a surefire giveaway that you are not so subtly moving on intellectually instead of spending quality time with the family.

## The Power of Presence

Presence is a powerful tool in bringing perspective to pain. While studying in El Salvador, I had the privilege of paying a visit to a group comprised of the mothers of children who had "disappeared" during the Salvadoran civil war.[3] The group, named *CoMadres*, engaged in advocacy and support for one another and for every mother who had lost a child during that brutal conflict. Among many other powerful things they told us, they shared with us their love and admiration for the former Roman Catholic archbishop of El Salvador, the late Oscar Romero. One mother said that they were most impressed with him because in spite of all of the responsibilities of his high office, he took the time to sit with them and pray with them. Sometimes, this mother said, he cried with them. For this, they said, they will always love him, although he had been assassinated fifteen years earlier. The ministry of presence generates volumes of material with which the preacher can approach any text.

Presence is also a powerful tool for evangelism. Millie Tanner was an usher and a relatively new member of the church. She often spoke of her family: a husband, a young adult daughter, and two elementary-aged grandsons. She frequently expressed how she longed for the day when her family would come to church, but she nonetheless worked diligently in the ministry. No matter when or for what purpose the doors of the church were open, Millie was there. She served food during fellowship meals, she attended Bible study, and she gave; Millie was a faithful member.

One day she informed me that her daughter, Diana, had given birth to a son, but the birth was dangerously premature. Millie asked me to pray. Not only did I pray, but also I visited the baby, and there in the hospital I met Diana. Week after week, that baby stayed in the Neonatal Intensive Care Unit (NICU), and week after week I visited. Sometimes I would encounter Millie, many times I would encounter Diana, and occasionally I met Diana's two sons. One day, however, what we all dreaded came to pass; the baby died. Everyone in the church was distraught. Millie's family was devastated. I went to Millie's home and sat with the family. Together we undertook the tragic task of planning a funeral for a newborn. The day of the funeral came, and I watched with grief as the mortician reached into the back seat of the car and picked up a small rectangular box covered with white brocade cloth. It was the casket of little John.

The funeral went as smoothly as possible for such a sad day, and the following Sunday, Millie's husband, Diana, and Diana's two sons all joined the church. Presence brought perspective to the pain of this family. From my presence they concluded symbolically that God in Christ was with them through their awful struggle, and so they committed themselves to God. This ought to be one of the chief aims of Christian preaching of any sort: to affect the listeners to the extent that through incarnated love and demonstrated spiritual power, they feel compelled to make a commitment to Christ.

---

**NOTES**

1. Peter M. Wherry and Wanda H. Wherry, *A Door of Hope: A Devotional with Sermons and Songs of Hope* (Keene, TX: Helping Hands Press, 2000), 33.

2. The lecture was delivered in the former site of the Hampton Ministers' Conference at Hampton University, Ogden Hall, circa 1990. Dr. Forbes was the conference lecturer on homiletics, and the text he used to elucidate the emphases of his lecture was Luke 4:18. It was one of the most profound and ministry-altering experiences in the more than thirty years I have been attending the Hampton University Ministers' Conference.

3. I studied in El Salvador in 1995, just two years after the end of the Salvadoran civil war, and remember vividly the danger we faced from US-backed Salvadoran death squads, which were still prevalent at that time.

I was privileged to have stood on the spot on which Oscar Romero was killed. Etched in my memory is the last statement of the sermon he was preaching when he was shot on Monday, March 24, 1980, in the chapel of San Salvador's Hospital de la Divina Frovidencia: "*Se me matan, yo resusito' en los pobrecitos salvadoreños*" ("If they kill me, I will be resurrected in the poor people of El Salvador"). His words are a prophetic reminder that presence always requires some level of sacrifice.

▪ CHAPTER 2 ▪

# The Funeral as Teachable Moment

## Everything plus the Kitchen Sink

*Jesus was a teacher. Among his other essential roles in the course of doing his Father's business, Christ focused on providing his followers with a blueprint for living . . . and with a vital challenge to apply Jesus' teachings as the only method for building a solid foundation for earthly and eternal life.*[1]

THE FORMER DEAN OF THE SEMINARY at Virginia Union University, the late Dr. Paul Nichols, often reminded us of the old adage that the scholar is not the person who knows all the answers. The true scholar, he said, is the person who knows where to find the answers. As a pastor, I have been adamant for many years that the most abundant setting for learning in the guild of ministry is the funeral. It is a venue for inquisitive preachers to find rich repositories of answers to many of the deep issues and questions of ministry. As a result, I have strongly suggested (and sometimes required) that apprentice ministers accompany me during the process of preparing for funerals. When a pastor conducts a funeral, every skill she or he has learned will be put to the test. Funerals are learning opportunities not only for the apprentice, but for the pastor as well. Any experience with such a textured and varied list of responsibilities must by definition create a teachable moment for all involved.

## Families Are Complex Systems

One of the first teachable moments relative to conducting funerals is that, during the process, the pastor must be a counselor. Depending upon the circumstances of the death, the pastor must be prepared to provide spiritual guidance to individuals and families within the circle of the deceased. To meet counseling responsibilities with excellence, pastors would do well to have a working understanding of Bowen Family systems theory. This does not require that every pastor be certified in social work or credentialed in psychology. It does mean that an effective pastor must understand the dynamics and mechanics of relationships in families.

Bowen Family systems theory presumes that families are necessarily and by nature interdependent. There are times, depending upon the intensity of the relationships between family members, that certain members of the family seem to each have one arm in the same emotional coat. That is, some members of the family not only share the same sorts of feelings, which is not surprising, but also things happen between two or more individuals that create a private constellation of complex responses to stress and grief.

Having even a basic understanding of how these relationships work is vital to bringing perspective to pain. One will never understand the pain of a family due to the death of a loved one until one understands the complexity of these relationships. The rub is, unless the family is known prior to the death in the family, the pastor has only a limited opportunity to observe and evaluate these dynamics, inasmuch as the interval from the moment of death to the funeral usually is a matter of days. Besides, even if the family is well-known to the pastor, funerals always bring together distant or extended members of the family a pastor may never have met. This means that a pastor must intentionally develop keen skills of observation and cultivate a useful lexicon of terms and concepts that inform the task at hand.

In figure 1, the eight tasks of systems theory are laid out in such a way as to suggest a relationship between them, but no linear process by which all the tasks must be accomplished. All of the tasks exert influence upon the family system, but no one of them is preeminent. The process is as individualized and unique as each family.

FIGURE 1: Components of Bowen Family Systems Theory

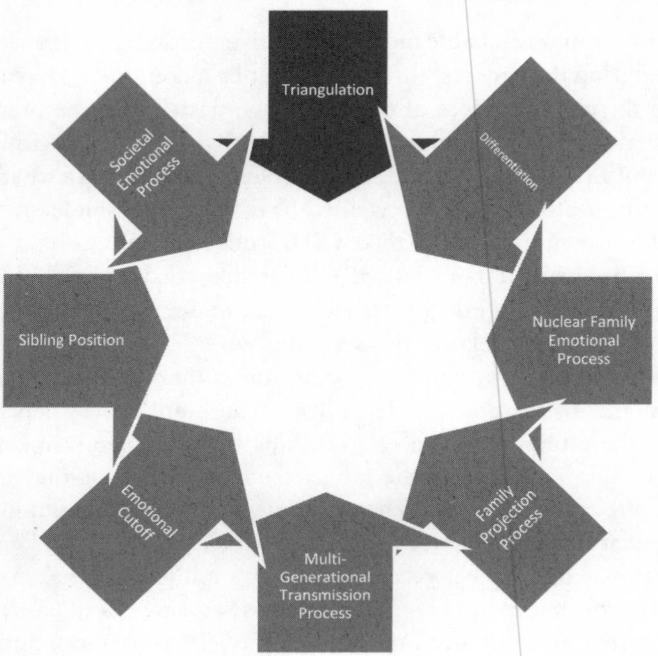


## Components of Bowen Family Systems Theory[2]

Death can debilitate a family. Death is fraught with difficult and divisive issues. There is planning to be done, and there are persons who fail to carry their weight in that planning. There are bills to be paid, and there are persons who lack resources to meet those obligations. There are also persons who have the resources to meet funeral obligations but refuse. There are insurance policies around which complex beneficiary questions arise. There are overwhelming feelings of grief, anger, and denial, and there is enormous stress related to these feelings. Further, one has no way to know in advance which family members are experiencing which of these feelings. Being able to understand and identify patterns and possibilities of triangulation will accelerate the pace at which the pastor is able to engage healthily the overarching process of grief and the stages of grief which underlie it.

## Triangles and the Pastoral Presence

One of the key systems terms in this context is "triangulation." Triangulation takes on many forms, but in families it generally refers to the practice of drawing a third person into a conflict or relationship which is originally between two people (often siblings). The third person becomes the channel of communication between the two dysfunctional people.[3]

One of the prime moments for communication breakdowns in families is during a time of grief. Being on the lookout for such breakdowns and for instances of unhealthy triangulation is vital to the pastor seeking to discern the meanings of unspoken and esoteric communication among family members. The ability to recognize triangulation and to enter the triangle strategically may allow the pastor to become a symbolic part of the family, sometimes permanently.

Let me acknowledge that triangulation often has a negative connotation. In most instances, the concept infers some attempt to remedy a dysfunction or problem and usually involves accomplishing the goal by exploiting the resources of some other entity. In military science, to triangulate is for marksmen to lock in on a target with overwhelming force by posting three shooters in various locations, thus ensuring that each bullet will do damage from its own vantage point, and between the three marksmen, a lethal shot will be the result. In politics, triangulation refers to the somewhat Machiavellian idea of usurping the ideas of an opponent in order to curry favor with the opponent's constituents, thereby rendering the opponent ineffective. In the social sciences, triangulation frequently refers to the fact that one partner in a two-person system draws another person into the system and uses the third person as a vehicle for communication when communication between the original two has deteriorated or ceased.

A somewhat comical example of this from movies or television is when a married couple has been arguing. The spouses are sitting in the same room with each other, but angry and refusing to speak. The wife looks at one of the children and says, "Tell your father it's time for dinner." The husband with a scowl looks at the child and says, "Tell your mother I'm not hungry!" Triangulation can and sometimes does involve this unhealthy strategy of leveraging a third person to facilitate communication between unwilling or recalcitrant parties. In the context of a pastor's involvement with a family during a time of death, however, triangulation can be the positive result of a pastor being drawn into and infusing a family system with renewed and much-needed vitality when the family is functioning at diminished capacity.

FIGURE 2: Triangulation

This dynamic is illustrated in figure 2, in which a triangle exists in the form of three gears. Without the third gear labeled "pastor," the other two gears will turn, but they will lack the synergy, efficiency, and dynamism that are possible. Once the energy from the third gear is included in the system, one family member can use the momentum of the pastor, and the pastor's momentum will inevitably add energy to the other two to turn in their own directions.

## Can Anything Good Come Out of Triangles?

Mrs. Glenda Scott, one of the elderly members of our church, approached me during the period of fellowship in worship. She handed me a crumpled note on a page torn from a small notepad. On the sheet, she explained, was the location and name of her older sister, who lay very ill in a nursing home. Mrs. Scott's request was simple: "Please go to see her, lay your hands on her, and explain to her that she does have a reason to live." I assured her that I would go. Soon after, I called Mrs. Scott and felt led to ask if she and her husband would be there when I arrived. She informed me that they did plan to be there. Mrs. Scott had been the lone caregiver to her sister throughout her lengthy illness.

When I arrived at the nursing home, Mrs. Scott had lined up several chairs along one wall of the tiny room. Only she and her husband were there. She sat by the bedside of her sister, whom I could tell had begun to make the transition to the other side. There were no respirators or other life-support devices attached to her. She was peaceful but absolutely unresponsive. Her face was turned away from us toward the wall, and the placid and still affect about her made it seem almost as if she had already gone. I sat by the bedside with the Scotts and talked with them about this dying sister. As I laid my hand on the sister's shoulder from time to time, we discussed the good times and the times of conflict between them. We even discussed their children. Several times, Mrs. Scott leaned over tenderly and spoke to her sister. I could tell from the increased volume of her voice that she feared her sister might not be able to hear her loving words. Mrs. Scott seemed to me to be concerned about the level and even the possibility of communication between them in this crucial time.

When the time was right, I joined hands with Mr. and Mrs. Scott and laid a hand on the shoulder of Mrs. Scott's dying sister, and we prayed together. I asked God for peace and for strength both for the Scotts and for this sister. I asked God to allow the dying sister to rest in the assurance that God would handle all of the unfinished affairs of this life. (Mrs. Scott was convinced that her sister would not "let go" until she heard once again the voice of her only son, whom she loved with all her heart.) At the conclusion of the prayer, Mrs. Scott and her husband sang, *a capella*, an old meter hymn called "It Will Be All Right." It was a moving and powerful moment. I left after about an hour. The time was around 5:30 p.m.

The next morning, Mrs. Scott called me to report that sometime in the wee hours of the morning, her sister had indeed "let go." She was happy that we had held our bedside prayer meeting, and she mused that it was divine providence that had brought us all together that day. She felt that, although her sister had not spoken, had been blind, had been immobile in illness—somehow, her sister had participated as we had talked, prayed, and sang.

While eternity may be the venue at which we learn the answer as to whether that dying sister in fact participated in the gathering that day, of this I am certain. For Mr. and Mrs. Scott, communication between them and their dying sister was enhanced by the triangle formed when they, the sister, and I came together. The enhanced energy, optimism, and joy—reflecting Jesus' teaching that where two or three gather in his name, he is present (Matthew 18:20)—are the true value of triangulation of this sort. The evidence of a pastor's involvement may seem at times opaque and unnoticed, but if we enter the family system properly, especially during a time of death, the outcome can be powerful and life-affirming.

## Grief in Pastoral Perspective

Grief is the primal, personal sorrow which grows out of a perception of loss.[4] Grief is not analytical, and it is not logical; it is purely emotional. That is not to suggest that the person who experiences grief has lost the capacity to think; quite the contrary. Grief as a response to death is intense precisely because a person has a cognitive understanding of irrevocable changes in a cherished human relationship. Grief is emotional because feelings of helplessness are intensified inasmuch as even when a death is anticipated, those who remain alive rightly feel that they have no control over developing events. Grief is the nursemaid to depression, and if grief is suppressed or poorly managed, it often nurtures depression. A pastor must allow family members permission to experience the normative pain of grieving, and bringing perspective to that pain is to generate a healthy climate for empowered healing within the family. The desired outcome of empowered healing is creating a climate which allows people to reach a state of acceptance of the obvious facts while maintaining wholesome relationships within the family and a working faith in God.

### Depression

Depression is often clinically described as anger turned inward. When situations in life are at odds with the wishes of a person, he or she may detach from others or refuse affection. A depressed person may withdraw from activities that once had been pleasurable, or that person may feel tired. Situational depression is usually transitory, and if a person is allowed to go through it, depression can pass on its own. However, the pastor and the church family need to be aware of the signs of depression. In this context, the theological, spiritual, and social engagement of the community of faith is an invaluable resource for creating a healthy climate for grieving persons to pass through the valley of depression.

## Anger

Anger has been described as the response to a blocked wish. Elisabeth Kübler-Ross has included anger as one of what she understood as the organic stages of grief,[5] and especially among religious families, experiencing anger during a time of death often generates enormous guilt and confusion. Whatever the form anger assumes, it is often a source of guilt among family members because many people view anger as impertinence or disrespect toward God. Numerous theological and homiletic opportunities emerge from angry feelings. A pastor must be expert in addressing these feelings to articulate that God is not insulted, nor is God diminished by these feelings, and God can lovingly handle even the rawest of these emotions.[6]

Denise Dombkowski Hopkins describes the response of ancient Israel to seasons of stress, loss, pain, and oppression as *chutzpah*.[7] Moreover, she outlines that particularly in the Psalms, there is a *chutzpah* tradition, which finds Israel "shaking the fist" at God as they grapple with understanding why such sorrow could befall God's chosen people. Every pastor must be on the lookout for family members who, in their own way, are shaking the fist at God. Many times, this anger surfaces as subtle hostility toward the pastor or toward the church. Sometimes, this anger surfaces in the form of a family member who refuses to join the family and pastor in prayer as a home visit concludes. In any event, people doing the difficult work of responding to a death in the family are grappling with a reality which, if they had their own way, they would reject, and they will never be able to find a healing perspective on their pain unless they are allowed to experience the depths of it. They need to know "it's okay; God can take it."

## Bargaining

Bargaining is the process by which an individual tries to negotiate, usually with God, for more time. In the case of grieving family members, this usually happens near the end of a serious illness of a loved one. "I'll stop smoking. I'll start going to church. I'll give more to charity. I'll be a better parent, better child, better friend." The logic is that God may intercede if only the survivor will commit to some personal life change in exchange for more time with a loved one. Ironically, despite being an intellectual exercise, bargaining may be the most irrational of all of the stages of grief because it is based upon the premise that the illness of a loved one and the behavior of the one doing the bargaining are somehow related. "God, if you will just give Grandma a little more time, I promise I'll stop drinking."

## Denial

Denial is a defense mechanism designed to minimize intellectually the impact of any circumstance on the human psyche. Denial is also a coping tactic which strategically postpones stress until a time when the individual feels more emotionally able to process what are usually dire or sometimes threatening situations. Kübler-Ross defines denial as an irrational resistance to and rejection of the obvious facts. Denial does not, however, always involve irrational rejection of obvious facts—that, for example, our deceased loved one is not, after all, dead. Sometimes denial is used to compartmentalize tasks so that overwhelming demands can be met. In such instances, denial is a detour.

Consider this example from my own life. It was a typical third Sunday in May. We arrived home from church a little sleepy because we had gone out to dinner, enjoying a relaxed and productive day. We were happy with the way things had gone at church that Sunday: the music, the message, the attendance, the new members. Then the phone rang. It was my oldest sister, Gwen. The words she spoke are etched in my memory. "Peter, it's about Chee-Chee," her nickname for our mother. "I don't know. I've never seen her this sick before."

Mom had been hospitalized, and just a couple of days earlier, I had spoken to her. I had also spoken to her on the previous Sunday, which was Mother's Day. Our mother had been battling breast cancer for seven years, but we had all been informed that her initial surgery seven years earlier had gotten all the cancer. Mom was simply suffering, so she told us, from residual effects of the treatment.

My conversation with my sister was brief. Gwen said, "I think you'd better come." But I couldn't believe what I was hearing. My sister was telling me that she thought our mother was dying. I hung up and immediately called Mom's doctor. After I peppered him with questions, his words unbelievably echoed Gwen's: "I think this would be a good time to come."

My wife, Wanda, and I frantically conferred and began throwing things in suitcases for ourselves and for the children. Thirty minutes later, I called my youngest sister, Tanya, to inform her that we were about to get on the highway, and she responded serenely, "Good, because she's gone." I fell back in the chair, quietly stunned, and thought, "She's gone? Gone where?" I thought, "You can't mean . . . dead!" But that is exactly what she meant. I barked at her, "Tell the mortician not to touch her until I get there!"

We jumped into the car and took off driving the thousand miles to Memphis, Tennessee, from Norfolk, Virginia. An hour later, I looked at the road signs above the highway and realized that, despite the times I had driven the familiar route, this time I had driven more than sixty miles in the wrong direction! The stress and shock of the moment had temporarily blocked my memory of familiar roads; it had even temporarily blocked out my vision as I unconsciously navigated a vehicle with my family inside. I had been looking at the road signs but not seeing them. For me, denial had taken the form of a literal detour.

Denial can present itself as symptoms of shock. It can influence human behavior and human decision making to the extent that sometimes at funerals we see family members who appear to be unsteady due to mood-altering medicines, or even some who appear to be under the influence of alcohol or other drugs. It is denial in response to stress which will occasionally cause persons to experience moments of disorganization and forgetfulness. The pastor's role in these times is to be alert to the signs and behaviors of denial and provide stability by modeling to the family a compassionate connection to the awful fact that someone they love is dead. The mere sight of the pastor realistically and compassionately confronting the unthinkable issues of death is a powerful and reassuring reality. Modeling for a family that there are ways to function and move on is at times the only evidence that there is life on the other side of the destabilizing encounter with death.

## Family Matters

These destabilizing encounters are the pivotal moments when family members can become dysfunctional and channels of communication can be obscured or mutated. All of the situations above are relationship stressors and can cause communication between people to deteriorate. When this happens, sometimes a third person is drawn into the family system. Sometimes this is to reduce stress between the two who are failing to communicate with one another. Sometimes this is to develop the third person as a channel of communication because the first two people have given up on speaking with or relating to one another. Sometimes, as in the case of Mr. and Mrs. Scott, the family simply needs a guide into the unknown realm of communication between the living and the dying. The pastor must be prepared to minister grace to those who feel wronged, promote peace among those who are alienated from one another, or even help to bridge the gap between family members when they feel less than competent to communicate with one another in the uncertain times often posed by death.

For this reason, it is vital to discern upon the first phone contact with the bereaved which family member seems to be in charge of the planning. Exercise caution here, because many times the person making phone contact with the pastor is not the authorized decision maker. Authorized decision-makers may be a surviving spouse, oldest child, cherished friend, or even a more distant relative such as a cousin, niece, or nephew. He or she may only be assisting with some details; occasionally, an individual will portray falsely that he or she is in control. Especially if a pastor is not familiar with the voice on the other end of the phone, once the niceties and small talk have been completed, it is appropriate to ask, "Are you in charge of the arrangements, or should I speak with someone else?"

The pastor attaching securely to the authorized decision-maker usually brings stability to the family, because it generates the feeling that progress is being made and creates the sense of a modicum of normalcy. A surprising level of anxiety exists within a family until the pastor has engaged with the decision-maker. That contact creates, in a nominal way, the perception of security during a time when life really feels out of control. Most often, the person is in that position because the deceased put confidence in him or her based on age, stability, skill, or affection. In any case, that person is usually in the capacity of leadership because he or she has been endorsed in some way for the task.

Once some relationship between the pastor and the authorized individual has been established, this person can usually give the pastor insight about the character of relationships between immediate members of the family. This will require keen observation because the person in charge may not be aware of revealing the nature of these relationships. It will, instead, require that the pastor watch closely and listen carefully when introduced during the home visit. It will be impossible to learn on the spot all of the key family members and what their issues or personalities may be, but this person can provide somewhat of a crash course on the relationships close to the planning table. Watch for small reactions and eye contact with and between these family members (or the lack thereof), and listen carefully to what appear to be off-handed comments. These are usually packed with vital information.

## The Kitchen Sink Unclogged

The pastor serves in a variety of capacities during the process of planning funerals: administrator, event planner, editor, worship leader, public relations person, scholar, theologian, teacher—and oh! I almost forgot: preacher. All of these roles for a pastor in the context of death are different from church to church and from denomination to denomination, but some core aspects of each role are similar no matter what the church or creed.

### Administrator

The pastor as administrator must demonstrate early in the process that she or he is overseeing the process. This is not a hierarchical position from which to wield power. The pastor as administrator can delegate responsibility but must demonstrate authority. Remember that in the event of a death in the family, people sometimes feel lost, abandoned, and disoriented. In these times, they must be made to feel that their pastor is not disconnected from the details but is very much presiding over the process. Even church leaders who participate in the process of making visits to the family must be sure to relay to bereaved families that their actions also represent the pastor. The key to bringing perspective to the pain of those traveling through the passage of death and dying is to incarnate the reality that their heavenly Parent is in touch with their pain. The pastor's leadership is the incarnation of God's empathy.

## Event Planner

The pastor as event planner in these times must possess or develop skills in inherently knowing how to organize people in the uniquely church activity of fellowship as a catalyst for healing. (Depending on the church tradition, fellowship may be described as a repast, a reception, or a funeral luncheon.) Such moments are not only instructive but also are the true power of the church. In fact, in the earliest Christian churches, fellowship was the glue that held the church together. The pastor must understand what represents the healthiest aspects of fellowship in the course of a death in the family and then consciously lead, insisting on excellence and carefully monitoring the quality of the hospitality offered to bereaved families.

Attending to the details of hospitality does not require that the pastor be personally involved in the delivery of service. In many churches, however, people who serve in the kitchens can become territorial about their use, and authentic fellowship and quality service may suffer. The pastor has the opportunity as event planner to articulate clearly and compassionately a vision and principles for fellowship, and then set up a mechanism for ensuring those principles are practiced.

## Editor

People may soon forget what is done during moments of happiness, but they will long remember what is done during moments of grief or bereavement. The documents written during these times are intrinsically historical documents, and they will be referred to for years to come. The service program, the obituary, and the resolutions and letters produced for the funeral will become the primary source information with which families heal, and they will become the markers of family history in perpetuity. Memorial cards will be pressed into family Bibles and sealed into scrapbooks and photo albums. The impressions and messages that pastors allow to go out under the name of the church will continue to identify them long after the funeral is over. Thus, not surprisingly, in relation to the task of preaching funerals, every pastor needs editorial skills. These are to be differentiated from general reading skills such as those which every literate professional must possess. An editor must develop precise and accurate abilities in evaluating the syntax, organization, grammar, and even layout of printed or electronic documents.

## Worship Leader

The responsibility of the pastor as worship leader is often underestimated in its importance because it is assumed that irrespective of what the pastor does or does not do during a funeral, as long as the program is well-organized and printed, as long as church leaders are fulfilling their responsibilities, the service will succeed. In reality, it is the pastor whose presence in and conduct of the service most often creates the tone and emotional tenor of the moment which will define success. Success has been achieved when the family and friends have been afforded the opportunity for healthy grief and worship in a context of order and compassion. In too many funerals, preaching and worship are sabotaged by emotion, and the service morphs into something which centers around grief only. Pastors must make clear and observe fastidiously rules of order, according to their own faith traditions, for funeral worship services, and their bearing during the service should reflect these principles. Consider this painful lesson from my experience ("Open Mouth, Insert Foot").

### OPEN MOUTH, INSERT FOOT

Verneeta Black was a coworker of my wife, Wanda, and me. I was bivocational at the time, and we worked together at a psychiatric hospital for children. As it turns out, Verneeta's mother died. Her mom was a member of a church which did not at that time have a pastor, and Verneeta secured permission for me to conduct the service. As always, I did my best to prepare. On the day of the funeral, a Roman Catholic priest came to the study requesting to make remarks at the appropriate time, confiding that he had been the deceased's employer. I was delighted to have him participate in the service.

Things went well, and it appeared that the family received what they needed from the process. When I got home later that day, however, I received a phone call from my coworker, with whom my wife and I had been quite close. Verneeta angrily denounced me for allowing the priest to speak and revealed to me that for all the years her mom had worked for this man, he had been cruel and otherwise unjust to her. Having him speak at the funeral had ruined the family's opportunity to heal.

We lost our friendship with Verneeta because of this careless and crucial mistake. I learned from that experience that no funeral service should include impromptu expressions from any person not approved in advance by the family. Every aspect of the service, from the music to the list of persons giving remarks, must be carefully planned and monitored by the worship leader.

## Public Relations

Public relations is still a little-known imperative for churches in the age of the information superhighway. To reframe a statement about lies versus the truth frequently used by the late E. K. Bailey, a bad name will travel around the world before a good name puts her shoes on. It is not the sole responsibility of the pastor to manage public relations for the church. However, funerals are unique and singular occasions on which the pastor must bear the brunt of how the church projects its image.

During funerals, pastors are essentially the public relations face of the church. They must interact with the extended family of the deceased, who frequently come from far-flung corners of the country and will carry their impressions back to those places. The pastor must interact with members of a wider local community who may be coming into the church to support and comfort the family. The pastor must also interact with businesses via the funeral home entrusted with serving the family. All of these are high-visibility points of exposure for the church. The pastor's power to bring perspective to the family's pain is either diminished or enhanced according to how well the pastor responds to the responsibility of managing the church's image in these various situations. All of these interactions will reflect positively or negatively upon the family as well as the church. If the pastor has managed any of these points of exposure poorly, it will add injury to a family which is already struggling to recover from injuries they feel are inflicted upon them by death.

## Teacher and Scholar

It is a given that in most congregations, the pastor is resident scholar, theologian, and teaching elder of the church. Fortunately for the church, the pastor is no longer the only person who is likely to have training or even credentials in theology. The pastor, however, in times of death in the church, must demonstrate an applied, practical facility for making plain the difficult and complex issues of death and dying, the justice and mercy of God, and the eschatological implications of family circles being broken. There is nothing so useless as the fruit of education hanging so high that it cannot be picked from the tree by hungry, hurting people on the ground.

The pastor's charge, then, is to make truth about even the loftiest struggles of life accessible to the hungry and hurting without pretending to have answers for every question and without pretending to fill every uncomfortable questioning silence with her or his own wisdom. The fact is that there are many, many things which none of us understand. The pastor, as true scholar, must have sense enough not to pretend to know everything, but instead he or she must point mourners to where the answers are: the One who does have the power to tell us everything important enough to know. The pastor who brings perspective to pain must sometimes exhibit the wisdom to be quiet and sit with hurting people for a while.

Ironically, no pastor can bring perspective to pain or preach funerals with power until she or he has successfully understood and entered into relationship with the people, in all the nuanced and professionally demanding senses of this. Although the tasks as described here rightly seem complex, onerous, and perhaps even outside of the ability of the typical preacher, the reality is, preaching is done to people.[8] The preacher who does not love her or his hearers enough to try and understand them is probably a hireling (John 10:12-13) and not worthy of the paradoxical privilege of being an ambassador in chains (Ephesians 6:20).

**NOTES**

1. Lora-Ellen McKinney, *Christian Education in the African American Church: A Guide for Teaching Truth* (Valley Forge, PA: Judson Press, 2003), xi.

2. Bowen systems theory consists of eight principles: triangles, differentiation of self, nuclear family emotional process, family projection process, multigenerational transmission process, emotional cutoff, sibling position, and societal emotional process. For purposes of this writing, triangulation is focused upon, although other principles (e.g., differentiation, sibling position) may have some relevance to the subject matter at hand. However, to maintain thematic focus, this one principle is highlighted because of its more direct relevance.

3. Ernst Abelin, *Die Theorie der frühkindlichen Triangulation, Von der Psychologie zur Psychoanalyse* (*The Theory of Early Childhood Triangulation: From Psychology to Psychoanalysis*), in *Das Vaterbild in Kontinuität und Wandel* (*The Father Figure in Continuity and Change*), ed. J. Stork (Stuttgart: Fromann-Holzboog, Ruhr-UNI-Bochum/Thomas Bonnhoefer Gotteslehre, 1986), 45–72.

4. David Casarett, Jean S. Kutner, and Janet Abrahm, "Life after Death: A Practical Approach to Grief and Bereavement, *Annals of Internal Medicine* 134.3 (February 2001): 208–15, available at http://www.annals.org/cgi/reprint/134/3/208.pdf, 2001 (accessed February 17, 2011).

5. Elisabeth Kübler-Ross, *On Death and Dying* (New York: Macmillan, 1969), 50–81. Kübler-Ross outlines five stages of grief (denial, anger, bargaining, depression, acceptance). It should be noted that since her groundbreaking book, other scholars have either contested the theory or rejected it outright. My observation and experience have been fairly consistent with the stages as outlined by Kübler-Ross and her observation that there is no set order of progression through them. It is likely that a pastor will encounter all of the stages during the course of engagement with a grieving family, and the stages may not necessarily present in the order in which Kübler-Ross or this author outlines them. Some people experience only two or three stages. Grief is a very individualized process.

6. A helpful resource is R. F. Smith, *Sit Down, God . . . I'm Angry: A Grieving Father's Conversation with God* (Valley Forge, PA: Judson Press, 1997).

7. Denise Dombkowski Hopkins is a friend and was a mentor to me throughout my doctoral studies at Wesley Seminary in Washington, DC. Her *Journey Through the Psalms*, rev. and expanded ed. (St. Louis: Chalice, 2002) is a marvelous resource which examines the Psalter as a guide for prayer and assists the reader in exploring the deep emotions of life. Denise is a preeminent Old Testament scholar.

8. Dietrich Bonhoeffer in Richard Lischer, *Theories of Preaching: Selected Readings in the Homiletical Tradition* (Durham, NC: Labyrinth Press, 1987), 29.

· CHAPTER 3 ·

# Pastoral Perspectives on Death and Dying

## Leaping Lessing's Ditch

*One does not get discouraged for long, or try to place a time limit on God's help. Nor does one threaten to leave the will of God if hardships last "just one day longer."*[1]

A GERMAN POET, PHILOSOPHER, and theater critic, Gotthold Ephraim Lessing (1729–1781) made an indelible impact upon Christian theology despite the fact that in his own time, his work was vilified and many of his life's ventures failed. Lessing nonetheless became an undeniable influence on German literature and Christian theology. He was a child of the Enlightenment and argued, standing in the shadow of his clergy father, that reason is the only means by which anything can truly be known. For Lessing, the Bible was an unreliable sourcebook for religion, as was faith, because both were subject to human input and, therefore, human error. According to Lessing, the New Testament was unreliable as historical fact and especially unreliable as any revelation from God. Surprisingly to some, Lessing's work was not intended to destroy Christianity, but his expressed enterprise was the correction and rescue of Christianity from human corruption. Lessing argued that there is a "great ugly ditch" between what Christians believe and what is certain. It is this ditch which he said he could not cross, no matter how many times he tried.

Lessing's ditch has been the theological nemesis of pastors and families wrestling with death and dying ever since Lessing himself failed to jump it. How does one jump the ditch between what one believes and what appears to be certain? During times of death, leaping the great ugly ditch between faith and human reason is especially crucial. One cannot easily leap the ditch between broken, grieving hearts clinging perilously to faith and the stark reality of death, but it can be done. The answer to how it can be done lies within the homiletic traditions of the church, and the pastor preaching at a time of death must appropriate a solid theological and biblical framework for approaching the task. These homiletic traditions and the theological and biblical framework which undergirds them must be grounded in an unshakeable and explainable belief that death for the Christian is not the end of our story. The issue is not to suggest that pastors lack faith. Rather, in too many cases, the content of that faith is unintelligible, or worse, it is not usable to the uninitiated or even to the rank-and-file member in the pew. This chapter is an attempt to propose a biblical and philosophical way forward in the task of helping pastors to construct a practical theology of death and dying.

## Ready . . .

The funeral sermon and the eulogy are vehicles for retraditioning[2] the anthropology and eschatology of the church, a rare opportunity outside of the funeral process. In this retraditioning, the pastor and the church have the privilege of reshaping the fearful and often unhealthy attitudes of families surrounding death and dying. Retraditioning also allows the pastor and church as community to convey profoundly the power and healing resident in encountering death when one is surrounded by others previously delivered from the dark ditchbank of limited human understanding. If the funeral is a teachable moment for associate ministers and pastors (see chapter 2), it is a teachable moment for the church as community and the community at large when pastors are able to articulate an intelligible and practical theology of death and dying. The funeral sermon and eulogy, then, become exercises in healing homiletics, as well as didactic and transformative encounters between the church and the wider community.

The genius of the church is community and commonality. Community is the relational aspect of the church which rescues those who are lonely from the danger of isolation.[3] Commonality is a powerful and even mystical validation of faith, namely, that so many from diverse backgrounds and experiences have encountered faith and the God of faith in so many of the same ways that neither mere coincidence nor group delusion can explain it away. With these two principles, the community of the faithful and the inexplicable commonality of the community's encounters with God, faith becomes the facts. This book is the product of having sat at hundreds of bedsides, listening with bated breath and watching with rapt attention as the dying crossed over. Many times, their utterances about what they saw and the powerful, profound peacefulness with which they crossed over were identical. Hundreds of people from various backgrounds and different families, dying under radically different circumstances, remarkably often saw and felt the same kinds of things: angels, cool verdant gardens, long-dead family members, future events. As a pastor, one of the greatest privileges of ministry has been the blessing of being allowed to share this unusual journey of commonality with them. This is the "mystic sweet communion with those whose rest is won."[4]

The bridge which has carried to healing countless millions in the community called church is belief in the bodily resurrection of Jesus from the dead, and belief in the bodily resurrection from the dead of those in the community who have faith in him. Resurrection, however, is one of the main issues which left Lessing stranded on the ditchbank of reason and leaves many who grieve stranded there as well. The pastor who preaches funerals well must be able to leap the ditch with wing-footed confidence, or those in bereaved families and even others in the congregation will remain, to the detriment of the church, mired in the mud of human reason.

Remarkably, it is often preachers who wrestle with themselves and who wrestle with their own issues on the muddy and slippery bank of Lessing's ditch. I have witnessed preaching at funerals which betrays the sad reality that among clergy, there are fissures in faith and misunderstandings in message when it comes to what they believe about the implications of death. I have heard too much preaching at funerals which seems to hedge bets and apologize for what should be the church's unabashed faith in the fact that death is not the end of our journey. Too much preaching I have heard at funerals seems to fear offending those in the audience who may not believe as the church does. The faith community has nothing to prove! The fact is, the burden to disprove what the community commonly believes about this rests squarely on the shoulders of those who do not believe.[5]

## Set . . .

Timothy Keller, in his groundbreaking book *The Reason for God*, also places the burden of proof for the truth of the Bible and the reality of the miraculous (especially the resurrection) squarely on the shoulders of those who deny the veracity of them.[6] Unlike Christian apologists, Keller does not try to argue that the Bible is a historical fact book. He does argue, however, that the facts, inspiration, and truth of the Bible are unimpeachable when they are properly understood. Keller articulates with great effect, for example, that those who deny the reality of resurrection have missed some pivotal issues clearly supporting it. There are extrabiblical data and sociocultural facts which, when objectively considered, leave little doubt about the reality of the resurrection of Jesus.[7] To those skeptics, for example, who try to dismiss resurrection by assuming that the followers of Jesus, being grief-stricken after his death, wanted to believe he was risen, Keller explains that Jews, who constituted most of the early following of Jesus, did not believe in and had no notion of a singular resurrection or a resurrection of individual people. For Jews, resurrection was to be a national phenomenon.[8] It would, therefore, have been unheard of for a Jew to be accepting of such an event unless it happened.

For those who attempt to explain away the bodily resurrection of Jesus by suggesting that people in the ancient world were much more accepting of superstition and were, as a result, more accepting of unexplainable events like resurrection, a more thorough reading of history is in order. Jews, as well as the Jews and Gentiles who became the first Christians, were influenced greatly by Hellenistic (Greek) culture. The ancient Greeks believed that the physical body was inferior to the spirit, always decaying, and constantly degrading toward extinction. Consequently, they would have rejected out of hand any notion of coming back to the human body once the spirit broke free from it. To return via resurrection, or by any other means, would have been unthinkable in the ancient world.

The empty tomb is the other thorny subject for those who reject the bodily resurrection of Jesus. It cannot be overemphasized how vital the empty tomb is to the resurrection. That the tomb of Jesus was empty and that at least four witnesses saw it empty is a major difficulty for those who try to undermine or who struggle with believing the resurrection. In the ancient world, and especially among Jews, the testimony of two or three witnesses validated officially the veracity of anything.[9] Moreover, the tomb being empty and the numerous sightings of a living, walking Jesus outside of the tomb confirm the resurrection. Without the sightings, the empty tomb may have been the result of a theft of his dead body, or a hoax, but the sightings make concealing a hoax, even an elaborate one, an impossibility. Richard Nixon, a president of the most powerful and technologically advanced society the world has ever known, could not keep a mere burglary at Democratic National Headquarters a secret. How is it feasible, then, that poor, undereducated members of a society could cover up an event which contradicted their own two-thousand-year-old religion, challenged politically the most powerful nation in the world (Rome), and overturned the laws of human physiology? It would carry the phrase "conspiracy theory" to truly grotesque proportions.

The eyewitness accounts in addition to the empty tomb make it impossible for the resurrection to be a hoax because no group in the history of the world has been able to conceal anything of such magnitude. Jesus appeared to Mary Magdalene, to the Twelve, to the two on the road to Emmaus, and even to more than five hundred people at one time. If this had not been so, there were too many witnesses wandering around who were still alive at the time that Paul wrote his letter to the Corinthians.[10] These witnesses could have challenged Paul's claims as fraudulent.[11] The eyewitnesses to the resurrected Jesus, coupled with the empty tomb, leave on the shoulders of those who do not believe a heavy burden of disproving the resurrection.

Ironically, Lessing's struggle to leap the ditch between what one may know with the human intellect and the mysteries of faith is the struggle of every person who has experienced the death of a loved one. Leaping the ditch of doubt is especially the struggle of every pastor charged at a time of death with bringing perspective to believers whose faith is shaken or whose family buckles beneath the pain. In the end, all things biblical, especially resurrection, are issues of faith. Such things are bound to remain foolishness to those who do not believe, and no amount of analysis is likely to change that. The work of bringing perspective to the pain of death is at its root, then, a theological job. Every pastor and every preacher at a funeral must herself or himself become an eyewitness to the resurrection of Jesus.

## Leap!

We turned onto Scott Street in Memphis. It was the same route I had traveled a hundred other times over the years as my family went to my grandmother's church, or the many times we gathered at the funeral home owned by our cousin, Reggie, for the wake of a family member. Owens and Son Funeral Home was two blocks from "Muh-Dear's," my grandmother's, church. I knew this route by heart. We turned into the funeral home parking lot, and my heart pounded, my stomach sank, and I remember coaching myself silently that I had to keep it all together in front of my wife and the kids. We had not stopped driving for eighteen-and-a-half hours. We did not stop to sleep, and we barely stopped to eat. I had given our cousin, who was the mortician, strict instructions that he was not to touch my deceased mother until I got there. He complied with my request.

After my cousin and I greeted each other politely, I asked to see Mom. Because of our family connection, he allowed us access to the cooling room where Mom was kept until I would give my consent to embalm her.[12] Wanda was so supportive, watching me like a hawk to make sure I was all right and holding onto me so I would feel her love. I had dreaded this moment for the entire thousand miles from Virginia, and as we approached the door of the cooling room, I didn't know how I would react. As the door opened, my stomach felt like it had the first time I crested the highest slope of a rickety, wooden roller coaster. We peered into the dimly lit room, and there Mom lay just as she was when she was brought from the hospital the previous day. For the first time in my life, I saw my mother, bald from the cancer, wrapped in a sheet, cold and lifeless. It was a catharsis, but remarkably, it was a catharsis in a good way. I didn't break down; I didn't pass out; I didn't get sick. Instead, a peace washed over me like I had never experienced with any other death. This time, when confronted with the severing of the precious, earthly bonds between a parent and a child and after walking with scores of others to this same dark place, I now stood at my own ditch between what I knew (death) and what I believed (resurrection), and I was all right. I understood in that instant that my faith had become the facts, and what I believed was infinitely stronger than even the powerful things I was feeling. When I realized this, all in a moment . . . I leapt!

> There's a land that is fairer than day,
> And by faith we can see it afar,
> For the Father waits over the way
> To prepare us a dwelling place there.
> In the sweet by and by,
> We shall meet on that beautiful shore.
> In the sweet by and by,
> We shall meet on *that* beautiful shore.[13]

**NOTES**

1. Nicholas C. Cooper-Lewter and Henry H. Mitchell, *Soul Theology: The Heart of American Black Culture* (Nashville: Abingdon, 1991), 147.

2. David Lowes Watson, a prominent United Methodist scholar, introduced this term in his popular writings on covenant discipleship in the United Methodist Church. Watson modeled the program on the early class meetings of Methodists in eighteenth-century England and America. Covenant discipleship is a method of building fidelity in the day-to-day following of the teachings of Jesus by voluntarily engaging what Watson's wife, Gayle Turner-Watson, calls "friends in the faith" in accountability relationships. According to Watson, traditioning is a vital concept among churches with more congregational forms of church polity and worship, because it represents an intentional way for the church to assert its teachings and convey through generations its ecclesiology.

3. Dietrich Bonhoeffer, *Life Together*, trans. and with introduction by John W. Doberstein (New York: Harper and Brothers, 1954), 21.

4. This is a line from "The Church's One Foundation" (1866), with lyrics by Samuel J. Stone (1839–1900) and music by Samuel Sebastian Wesley (1810–1876). This hymn is in the public domain.

5. See Boykin Sanders's treatment of 1 Corinthians 15 as apocalyptic drama, "1 Corinthians," in *True to Our Native Land: An African American New Testament Commentary*, ed. Brian K. Blount, Cain Hope Felder, Clarice J. Martin, and Emerson B. Powery (Minneapolis: Fortress, 2007), 298–302.

6. Timothy Keller, *The Reason for God: Belief in an Age of Skepticism* (New York: Dutton, 2008), 209–21.

7. Numerous ancient sources outside of Christianity, most of them hostile to the faith, mention Jesus and his followers. Moreover, many of these sources mention the miracles and resurrection of Jesus, and they are not able to deny the miracles; rather, they decry them as sorcery. A partial list of such ancient writers includes Pliny the Younger (112 CE), the Babylonian Talmud (sixth century CE), and Toledoth Yeshu (sixth century CE). This last source mentions the empty tomb and that Jewish leaders found it empty. It also mentions that Jesus healed, performed miracles which are called "sorcery," and taught rabbis and many others who were believers and wrote documents which do not appear in the Christian canon.

8. See John 11:24. The Old Testament is replete with the Jewish understanding of national/communal resurrection as well (see Daniel 12:2). Those factions in ancient Israel that did believe in resurrection or life after death only understood the event to be impending in a communal sense.

9. See Deuteronomy 17:6; 19:15; see also Matthew 18:15.

10. See 1 Corinthians 15:3-6. Paul details most of the appearances of Jesus after the resurrection and adds a pivotal postscript: that most of the more than five hundred who saw Jesus alive were still living at the time Paul wrote his letter. Paul was the earliest of the New Testament writers, and if there had been any witness to refute Paul's testimony, surely none of the rest of the New Testament would likely have been written. Jesus and Paul would have been exposed as frauds, and the story would have been over.

11. Sanders, "1 Corinthians," 299.

12. An interview with a licensed mortician reveals that laws and practices have changed drastically over the past several years relative to allowing access for nonprofessionals to the previously esoteric domain of cooling rooms and morgues (embalming rooms) of funeral homes. During the time when my wife and I owned and operated a funeral home in Virginia, it was strictly forbidden for unlicensed persons to even look inside a morgue, much less walk into a cooling room or morgue. The interview with this licensed mortician (who also cited articles from professional journals in 2010) reveals, however, that there are now funeral homes in the United States which allow families to witness through plate glass the embalming of their family members. These types of access still vary from state to state. This radically open access is evidence of the striking changes that have developed in professional funeral services since my mother died in 1997.

13. Sanford F. Bennett (1836–1898) wrote the lyrics of "In the Sweet By and By" (1868), sometimes titled "There Is a Land That Is Fairer Than Day." The music is by Joseph P. Webster (1819–1875). The song is in the public domain. Emphasis is added.

· CHAPTER 4 ·

# Finding and Selecting the Text

## Texts under Negotiation

*The word arises out of the Bible, takes shape as the sermon, and enters into the congregation in order to bear it up. This self-movement of the word to the congregation should not be hindered by the preacher, but rather he should acknowledge it. He should not allow his own efforts to get in its way. . . . Upon Christ, however, who is the proclaimed Word, should fall all of the need, the sin and death of the congregation.*[1]

PREACHING IS UNIQUE FROM EVERY other form of written or spoken discourse in that it is first and finally spiritual and not semantic. The Holy Spirit is the catalyst, and in fact, the "closer" for every type of sermon—the One who speaks the Word. The Holy Spirit is, as well, the imprimatur of God on both the life and the praxis of the preacher. It is anointing from the Holy Spirit which affords the ability and power of the preacher to minister with compassion, discover the text for preaching, exegete with clarity, and deliver the message of the sermon or eulogy.

It is the work of the Holy Spirit which animates every aspect of the preaching enterprise; from text to context, it is the ongoing work of the Holy Spirit which makes preaching possible. Preachers at their own peril neglect or denigrate the involvement and importance of the Holy Spirit, but according to James Forbes, this is precisely the ailment of much modern preaching. For various reasons, communities of faith and the preachers who arise from them are plagued with the malady of what I call spiritual anemia. Spiritual anemia results in preaching that is perfect but powerless.

Such sermons are flush with substance but void of substantiality. Sermons which suffer from this malady do so owing to a lack of prayer and a failure to look upward for spiritual unction. Forbes references Rudolf Otto's notion of *mysterium tremendum* to support the assertion that there is, ironically, in much of Christendom and in preaching particularly, "emotional ambiguity" about engagement of and surrender to the Holy Spirit.[2]

The sermon in its purest and most powerful form must not be bound by personal or intellectual forensic agendas but must facilitate what Christ himself has initiated: incarnation. This cannot be done apart from the Holy Spirit. Christ must not be obscured by the preacher, but the preacher must, through the agency of the Holy Spirit and her or his authentic being, be an usher to the presence of Christ into the midst of hungry and hurting people. This understanding of preaching is at odds with manifestations of preaching we see on many Sunday television shows or even those examples of preaching found in some sermon compendia these days. On television, the 'Gospel of Prosperity' frequently trumps the Good News of Salvation, and the commercialization of preaching and worship often obscures the call to spiritual and existential transformation. Since the task of preaching is to incarnate Christ among people, the funeral sermon and the eulogy have a special affinity to this understanding of the preaching assignment.

For this reason, it is imperative that the preacher exercise special care in selecting the text, which is the foundation of any sermon.[3] If preaching is to be incarnational and textual, funeral preaching must conspicuously connect the presence of Christ to the "is-ness" of culture. This sort of preaching, whether on Sunday morning or during a funeral, will be not only redemptive but also transformative. "Transformation" here must be contrasted with the purely contemplative understanding of the term promulgated by some academics.[4] Transformation is the benchmark of success in connection with the funeral process; namely, does the church in its engagement with grieving people at least catalyze the movement of people from grief to healing? James Harris writes, "Worship should be oriented toward transformation—both spiritual and social."[5] There is no more appropriate time for persons to expect transformation than when they are grieving. Given such a spiritual imperative for funeral preaching, the finding and selection of a text for that preachment must also be spiritual endeavors.

## Spiritual Listening[6]

The seedbed of text discovery and selection is the encounters the preacher has with the family. Spiritual listening while having seemingly mundane conversations on the phone or in the home with a bereaved family creates an echo chamber in which the preacher may hear faint whispers of a text. The preacher must, of course, be predisposed to hearing the whispers by having a working knowledge of the Bible and a theological understanding of the broad themes of Scripture, as well as being able to identify what the late Miles Jones has referred to as "preachability."[7] Preachability in part refers to the ability of the preacher to discern the appropriateness of the content of a text based upon her or his improvisational skill in employing language through imagination, creativity, and symbolism. This improvisation, according to Jones, is not preaching without rules. It is the ability to dig into a text and reformulate language to address the events at hand in the text and in the community while creatively using gestures, music, and more to expand the ways people think about those events.

Spiritual listening can cause the preacher to visualize in a deceased Marine the "good soldier" spoken of by Paul to the young preacher Timothy, or to see in a woman who dies following a long illness the woman who touches the hem of Jesus' cloak as he walks along. Finding and selecting a text is at once the result of spiritual listening and diligent, creative preparation by the preacher. Spiritual listening is the indispensible pretext to the text and is the unavoidable preamble to finding the organizing principle[8] around which the preacher will gather the bereaved family and community for reflection on their condition of existence: death.

## Empathic Vision[9]

A crucial aspect of bringing perspective to the pain of grieving families, especially in the process of text location and selection, is modeling the reality that they do not grieve alone. Empathic vision presumes that the pastor or preacher is not so professionally disengaged from the pain of a family that he or she cannot or is not willing to participate in that pain. Questions often arise in pastoral care settings as to whether it is ever appropriate for a pastoral caregiver to cry with grieving families. The fact is, when a death occurs in the church, the family members of the deceased are not the only persons who have experienced a death. The pastor and church have also experienced a death. Even Jesus, at the grave of a deceased friend, wept (John 11:35).

There are some times when the most helpful and powerful thing a pastor can do is to weep with one who grieves. Resonating personally with the pain of others is a human, sometimes powerful, and uniquely pastoral response. Moreover, empathic vision creates a homiletic connection to the listeners which cannot be duplicated with mere theological or exegetical analysis. Text selection is directly affected by this. The emotional connection one experiences when grieving with people informs the perspective about what themes and content will be helpful to mourners because, in some sense, the preacher is herself or himself one of those mourners.

Preaching is always enhanced when it draws from a reservoir of real emotion. Nothing militates against effective preaching more than a preacher who approaches the task with dispassionate detachment. As the old saying goes, "Nobody wants an aspirin that ain't helping your headache." It should be noted, however, that there are ways of conveying real emotion other than with tears. If tears are shed, they should in no way communicate the sense that the pastor has lost control of the process. Whether at the hospital or other location at the time of death, in the home during a visit, or during the service, tears are appropriate, so long as they convey empathy and not self-indulgence.

## Preaching and Psychoanalysis

Finding and selecting the text will be greatly aided by drawing from the model of Walter Brueggemann concerning biblical interpretation.[10] Brueggemann utilizes strategies of psychoanalysis to develop an understanding of biblical interpretation, but these same principles can directly apply to the selection of a text for preaching as well. First, what have come to be known in psychotherapy as Freudian slips, or words or phrases that are odd or seem to be non sequiturs, are useful in surfacing the hidden, subterranean themes that carry within them possibility for the reimaging of life.[11] Likewise, in selecting a text, it may be the words, phrases, or names that seem oddly out of place which hold powerful potential for a transformative eulogy or funeral sermon. Teasing out of that which does not seem to fit in a text may, in fact, hold the key to unlocking a creative approach to even a well-known text. The preacher must pore over the esoteric details, ever on the lookout for those things which routinely go unnoticed as out of place.

In Matthew 27:52-53, at the death of Jesus the dead bodies of "God's people" (GNB/TEV) rose out of their graves. They lingered near their graves until after the resurrection, when they went into Jerusalem and many people saw them. Lots of interesting preaching can come from reflecting on the time between the dead leaving their graves on Friday and going into the city three days later.

In 1 Samuel 16:23, the text says that an evil spirit came "from God" and afflicted Saul. It almost goes unnoticed here that the evil mentioned explicitly comes from God. It could be helpful to examine how people wrestle with their perceptions of God's abandonment or abuse.

In 2 Timothy 4:10, the apostle Paul requests immediate assistance from Timothy, his son in ministry. Paul mentions Demas, who was a deserter; Titus, who was a well-known apostle; and Crescens, whose name appears only here in the New Testament. Great preaching can emerge from unearthing how one can achieve great things for God out of seeming obscurity.

Second, Freud understood the value of the details of a conversation, and according to Brueggemann, it is in these details that the power of a text lies, rather than in the obvious.[12] Value, transformation, and healing are likely to be most evinced in the funeral from engagement with texts which intentionally but carefully move people away from the monotony of customary fare. In the minute details of inflection, body language, facial expression, or gestures, conversation may evolve into a diametrically different communication than merely reading words printed on a page. In the minute details of a text, sometimes in details as specific as punctuation, implied pauses, and strategic repetitions, the preacher will discover pinpoint openings into the souls of grieving people.

It is important to note that inflections here refer to the English language, as opposed to Hebrew or Greek. Inflections in the English language can be perceived by paying attention to small words such as pronouns. These small words can wield powerful meaning in a text. In funeral preaching, pronouns personalize and draw God's actions toward the believer. Pronouns bring intimacy to the promises of God and ownership to the love and mercy of God. It is wonderful if one has had the privilege to study ancient languages, but knowing Hebrew, Aramaic, or Greek is not mandatory in order to preach well. A reliable and honest English Bible is the indispensible tool of the faithful preacher who may not have a grasp of biblical languages. Reliable translations can reveal the beauty and power of the details and nuances of a text and lift preaching beyond what is obvious.

For example, in Psalm 23:1 (GNB/TEV), God is not shepherd in a deistic, detached way. "The Lord is *my* shepherd. I have everything I need." Or, in Matthew 28:20, Jesus, in personal and reassuring tones, promises his continued presence with the believers he is about to leave behind. Powerful preaching can emerge from the promise of presence specified by the pronouns of this text.

Third, unearthing and presenting the new material of a text is not sufficient to bring about healing or transformation. New material refers to texts or portions of texts which, because of obscure phrases or expressions, may not be frequently preached. Examples of such obscure or new material with little transforming value in a funeral sermon include Zephaniah 3:16, in which a little-known Semitic expression is used to demonstrate the effect of fear. The text warns, "Do not let your hands hang limp" (GNB/TEV). Or, in Judges 3:12-22, God sends Israel a deliverer from the oppression which was the result of their unfaithfulness to God. Ehud, the deliverer, stabs the obese Moabite king, Eglon; the knife's handle is concealed in the folds of fat, allowing the assassin to escape.

Selection of texts for shock value or to satisfy a need for attention will not assure that the chosen text will make sense or bring about healing and transformation. The preacher, like the psychoanalyst and patient who are engaged in therapeutic conversation, must brood over the sights, sounds, and contrasts and "walk around"[13] the new material until the hard work of interpretation is done.

Fourth, just as Freud described in the organic structure of the ego, human beings have a need to censor and repress some memories and information about the self in order to be an integrated, functioning individual. So it is with humankind attempting to grasp a workable understanding of God. In order to be able to process the enormity of God, or at times the uncomfortable justice of God, the radical righteousness of God, or even the disarming love of God, the exegete at times gravitates to a censored, filtered, homogenized text. Such a text is full of broad themes and usually adheres to the familiar and benign, but it may leave out key, revealing, perhaps shocking aspects of God. Brueggemann advocates a willingness to confront the often-ignored texts in the same way as "recovered memories" are confronted in psychotherapy. According to Brueggemann, in psychotherapy, "new life is mediated through the recall of painful, unresolved hurts and wishes."[14] The recovered memories of those painful, unresolved things facilitate a reimaging of the traumatic and recovered. That is, painful, traumatic content in texts can facilitate a similar process of reimaging in preaching to the bereaved. Such texts can facilitate the reimaging of life in the bereaved as hearers as well.[15] Just as "telling" is a powerful tool in reimaging life for victims of abuse, proclaiming the mournful, unpleasant messages in certain texts can help hearers reclaim power and reimage life after the death of a loved one.

Preaching laments from the Psalms and book of Lamentations can be a powerful way of recovering and reimaging the painful passages of life. Laments can help hearers to confront the sometimes perplexing realities of being God's people in a context of pain. Luke Powery argues that there can be no praise or joy without lament. In fact, in the Psalms, "what concludes in praise does not begin in praise."[16] Some wonderful examples of laments for homiletic telling sessions are Psalms 35, 69, 88, 109, 137, and 140.

## The Importance of Literary Genres

Inasmuch as text selection for preaching concerns identifying a biblical text, it is reasonable to ground the process in creatively canvassing the sourcebook, the Bible, for suitable material. Numerous strategies are extant, but winnowing out the thousands of disparate possibilities by literary genre is a logical first step. Old Testament genres include foundational myths and legends, legal codes, genealogies, annals, prophetic books, prayers or laments, proverbs, wisdom, and apocalypse. All of the Old Testament genres can be further subdivided into more specific categories.

In the New Testament there are the Gospels and Acts (narrative), letters, and apocalypse. Sometimes the letters are further subdivided into more specific headings such as church orders (1 Timothy,

Titus), testament (2 Timothy, 2 Peter), sermon (Hebrews), wisdom collection (James), and encyclicals[17] (1 and 2 Peter).[18] Within the Gospels there are parables, aphorisms or proverbial sayings, pronouncement stories, miracle stories, and discourses (e.g., the "I am" sayings in the Gospel of John). In Acts there are adventure narratives. In the epistles there are poetic exhortations (vice and virtue lists), admonitions, poetry, and hymns. Form-critical approaches to text selection, among other things, can help the preacher to make preliminary decisions about the content of the sermon based upon the form of the text.[19]

If, for example, the deceased was a person whose death came, as do many, despite prayers for supernatural healing, preaching a miracle story during the eulogy or funeral sermon may be a good counterintuitive approach in which the sometimes painful "recovered memories" of death are refracted and reimaged.[20] Reimaging in this context could lead the hearer to understand the disappointment that God seems to have not answered prayers for healing. It could mean that God did, in fact, answer, but not in the ways that we in our grief and finite humanity imagined.

Miracle stories, then, lend themselves to grappling with the events in life which are at odds with the plans, hopes, prayers, and goals of people. Theologically speaking, such experiences may be perceived as "death-dealing" events. Milton Crum, in his analysis of "Scripture as story," explains that "Story is the chief medium for the revelation of God in history."[21] When preparing a funeral sermon or eulogy using a miracle story, the preacher would do well to remember the three basic questions of preaching literary forms as posed by Mike Graves:

1. What is the text saying?
2. What is the text doing?
3. How can the sermon say and do the same?[22]

Miracle stories preached at funerals, therefore, can revisit the painful and disappointing experiences of life and through creatively retelling the story, reimage them from death-dealing struggles into life-giving encounters with the power of God in Christ.

The form of a text has much to say about what the mood of the text is, and therefore, what the mood of the eulogy or funeral sermon will be. It is not a foregone conclusion, nor should it be, that the mood of funeral preaching is funereal. There are times when it is appropriate for preaching at a funeral to be laced with humor. The form of the selected text will significantly inform the mood of the preaching. The mood established by a lament from the psalms, for example, would be different from the mood established by the narrative in Acts 20:1-12, where a young man bored by Paul's preaching dies by falling out of a window. Allow the text, its form and content, unhindered, to set the tone. In this way, the presence of the risen Christ is free to catalyze changes in affect and understanding and becomes the agent by which the Word enters into the congregation. As the Word enters the congregation, just as light banishes darkness, the need, the sin, and death of the congregation are in some ways displaced as well.

Transformation from grief to recovery is always a process, but faithful preaching which handles with excellence the forms of the text, and thereby the mood of the message, wields the power of change and, as such, the power to call those exiled to the dark places of grief back home to receive the "oil of gladness instead of mourning" (Isaiah 61:3 NRSV). It is unavoidably true that no place Jesus ever entered and no person Jesus encountered was ever able to remain the same again. This transformational engagement with hurting people through careful attention to text selection, form, and, therefore, content is consonant with Jesus' understanding of his own praxis:

> The spirit of the Lord God is upon me,
>     because the Lord has anointed me;
> he has sent me to bring good news to the oppressed,
>     to bind up the brokenhearted,
> to proclaim liberty to the captives,
>     and release to the prisoners;
> to proclaim the year of the Lord's favor,
>     and the day of vengeance of our God;
>     to comfort all who mourn;
> to provide for those who mourn in Zion—
>     to give them a garland instead of ashes,
> the oil of gladness instead of mourning,
>     the mantle of praise instead of a faint spirit.

They will be called oaks of righteousness,
  the planting of the LORD, to display his glory.
They shall build up the ancient ruins,
  they shall raise up the former devastations;
they shall repair the ruined cities,
  the devastations of many generations.

—ISAIAH 61:1-5 (NRSV)

**NOTES**

1. Dietrich Bonhoeffer in Richard Lischer, *Theories of Preaching: Selected Readings in the Homiletical Tradition* (Durham, NC: Labyrinth Press, 1987), 29.

2. James Forbes, *The Holy Spirit and Preaching* (Nashville: Abingdon, 1989), 20–23. *Mysterium tremendum* is a term which describes the simultaneous thrill and dread of encounter with God.

3. Although it is understood that there are topical sermons, sermons which are textual are most appropriate for funerals. More is written on this point in chapter 5.

4. Dietrich von Hildebrand, *Transformation in Christ* (Manchester, NH: Sophia Institute Press, 1990), 105–47. The book was first published in 1940 under the pen name Peter Ott due to Nazi threats. It was later translated into English by Hildebrand's second wife, Alice, and published by Longmans in English in 1948. For Hildebrand and others in the Roman Catholic theology of the time, contemplation is superior to action. The liberation theologies, both Roman Catholic and black, which emerge some fifteen to thirty years after Hildebrand first published this work greatly and rightly expand the notion of what transformation is.

5. James H. Harris, *Pastoral Theology: A Black Church Perspective* (Minneapolis: Augsburg Fortress, 1991), 90.

6. This is an intrinsically homiletic skill which holds in tension Augustine's explanation of *uti* (the use of a thing) and *frui* (the blissful penetration of a thing). Spiritual listening is a term I have coined to describe an action which intentionally appreciates in moments of simple presence and engagement with others opportunities for inspired preaching. Spiritual listening also presupposes that the preacher not be emotionally absent from the grieving family while engaged in a navel-gazing homiletic exercise. It is listening with empathy and purpose. Like any other skill, spiritual listening must be cultivated and practiced in order for the preacher to achieve maximum facility in its application (compare the first book of Augustine's *De doctrina christiana* with *De civitate Dei* 19.10).

7. Miles Jones, *Preaching Papers: The Hampton and Virginia Union Lectures* (New York: Martin Luther King Fellows Press, 1995), 55.

8. The organizing principle is the technical term for the thesis statement, or the distillation of an expository sermon into one or two sentences. This

is the device which provides thematic focus in expository preaching as Miles Jones taught it.

9. Empathic vision is a term I have coined to describe the preacher's ability to connect with others. It speaks directly to the manner in which the preacher sees the grief being experienced by a family. To say that the preacher possesses empathic vision presumes that the preacher has the capacity to experience grief with others. In this way, the preacher not only feels for a grieving family as an overly objective third party but also feels with them almost as a member of the family.

10. Walter Brueggemann, *Texts Under Negotiation: The Bible and the Postmodern Imagination* (Minneapolis: Augsburg Fortress, 1993), 59–61.

11. Brueggemann, *Texts Under Negotiation*, 59–60.

12. Brueggemann, *Texts Under Negotiation*, 60.

13. Brueggemann, *Texts Under Negotiation*, 60.

14. Brueggemann, *Texts Under Negotiation*, 60.

15. Brueggemann, *Texts Under Negotiation*, 60–61.

16. Luke A. Powery, *Spirit Speech: Lament and Celebration in Preaching* (Nashville: Abingdon, 2009), 23.

17. An encyclical is also a letter, but it is a more stylized version of a letter which was disseminated as a circular, that is, a letter designed for a broader audience. An epistle, by contrast, was a letter which dealt with spiritual or theological issues but was intended for a particular church or ecclesial context.

18. Felix Just is one scholar who has identified such literary genres, and although his categories reflect a somewhat Roman Catholic bent, they make sense in terms of preaching and are more specific than what is traditionally espoused.

19. Mike Graves, *The Sermon as Symphony: Preaching the Literary Forms of the New Testament* (Valley Forge, PA: Judson Press, 1997), 19–25.

20. Brueggemann, *Texts Under Negotiation*, 60–61.

21. Milton Crum Jr. *Manual on Preaching: A New Process of Sermon Development* (Wilton, CT: Morehouse-Barlow, 1988), 98–107.

22. Graves, *The Sermon as Symphony*, 105–13.

▪ CHAPTER 5 ▪

# Sermon Structure in Funeral Preaching

## The Uncertain Sound

> *The word as the bearer of meaning has an impact on all sides of man's spiritual life, on the whole personality. It is addressed to the intellect; it informs man about his situation, his actual and ideal relation to God, the world, and himself. . . . The word speaks to the person as a whole, to the free, responsible, and deciding center of the person.*[1]

THE MATTER OF HOMILETIC STRUCTURE in funeral preaching is much more than an aesthetic consideration. Structure is connected directly to the agenda of the preaching in the same way that form follows function in the design of airplanes and automobiles. Aerodynamics is a crucial consideration when it comes to improving gas mileage in cars or ensuring that an airplane lifts from the ground and remains in the air during and after takeoff. In the same way, the sermon's form must follow function because human beings, the consumers of Christian preaching, are multifaceted, complex creatures who experience life spiritually, intellectually, existentially, dialectically, and volitionally. The form or structure of the sermon must in the end be determined by the text, the context, and the occasion.

Every occasion I have witnessed during which the preacher seemed to handle the preaching assignment poorly had as one aspect of the struggle the failure to organize the message coherently. There appears to be some debate in preaching circles about the proper structure for a eulogy or funeral sermon. The possibilities run the gamut, so much so that too many preachers miss the opportunity to preach with power, because the message is undercut by poor sermonic structure. At the outset it must be said that although the message is for a funeral, it is still preaching. For this reason, similar rules apply to Sunday morning worship and preaching at funerals. The message, whether eulogy or funeral sermon, must still be—must especially be—Good News.

## A Eulogy or a Sermon?

Throughout this book, the terms "eulogy" and "funeral sermon" have been employed when speaking in the abstract about funeral preaching. Each time one appears, so does the other as a suggestion of their mutual exclusivity. Eulogies may be preached for persons who are not members of the church, but people whom the preacher knows intimately are the most appropriate subjects for eulogies (see chapters 1, 6, 9, 11, 12, and 13). Brad Braxton writes,

> While a eulogy can attempt to do too much, it can also accomplish too little. A eulogy that accomplishes too little focuses more on the life of the deceased than on God. We derive the word "eulogy" from Greek words that mean "good word." Primarily, a eulogy should present the "good word" of God's presence, actions, and promises. Effective eulogies sensitively seek to include significant details from the life of the deceased. Yet, a eulogy's ultimate aim is to situate the life of the deceased and the hurt and hope of the mourners within the eternal framework of God's gospel.[2]

Attempting to preach a eulogy for an individual not well-known by the preacher may result in embarrassing errors and breaches of trust between the preacher and the family. The family may ask, behind their eyeballs (that is, in their minds), "Is the preacher trying too hard to be familiar with us, and if so, what is the ulterior motive?" They may wonder, "Is the preacher trying to play on our emotions by pretending to know things that she or he does not know?" The family may also ask, "Doesn't she or he even care enough to get the facts about our loved one straight?" In the last case, families may leave the service feeling overlooked and neglected because the preacher was too uncaring to learn about them and characterize accurately someone they love. Worse, the preacher may come across as disingenuous and even dishonest, and in that case, trust from the family toward the preacher has been compromised, sometimes irretrievably so. Don't forget, people will long remember the things done to and for them during a time of grief and bereavement.

The simplest distinction between a eulogy and a funeral sermon is that in the eulogy, the details of the life of the deceased are known to the preacher. In the funeral sermon, the details of the life of the deceased are generally not known, or at least there has usually been no close relationship between the preacher and the deceased. (As in any life situation, there are sometimes exceptions to this rule.) In a eulogy, then, the 'good word' is preached as specific details from the life of the deceased and the grief of the mourners are linked in the context of God's love and provision for those who love and believe in Christ. In the funeral sermon, the preacher usually does not know intimately the details from the life of the deceased, so he preaches Good News and compassion to the living. If done well, the mourners derive comfort from making their own personal connections between the message and the life of the deceased.

## One of a Kind

Just as every deceased person is a unique individual and every family is comprised of unique people, so no two funeral sermons should be the same. There is, therefore, no one proscribed structure for preaching these events. Certain sermon structures, however, do lend themselves more easily to addressing the lives of people in meaningful ways. For example, perhaps the death in question has caused some unusual soul-searching in the family, either because a person died under questionable circumstances or because the death has caused family members to question their faith in specific ways, such as after the death of an infant or child.

In these cases dialectical structure may prove most effective.[3] Dialectical preaching is useful in developing the difficult discipline of homiletic originality, in large part because its relevant question allows for every sermon to be as unique as the people for and to whom it is preached (for an example, see chapter 6). The structural elements of the dialectical method provide an analytical framework for examining issues from multiple perspectives and require the preacher to rely on her or his own analysis to arrive at a synthesis of the matter at hand. The dialectical method or structure, as advanced by Samuel DeWitt Proctor, consists of six main components:[4]

1. Proposition: the sermon summarized in a sentence or two.
2. Subject: essentially, the sermon title.
3. Thesis: a statement of an ideal or desired condition; describes how life *should* be. (This often functions as the Introduction to a sermon.)
4. Antithesis: a statement of the real condition; serves as a counterpoint to the thesis and highlights the obstacles in attaining the ideal. (This may be included as part of the Introduction.)[5]
5. Relevant question: a doorway to the body of the sermon; creates a "need to know" in the minds of the hearers.
6. Synthesis: encompassed in the body of the sermon; it answers the relevant question and bridges the gap between ideal and real.

As do other forms of preaching, the dialectical method begins with thematic focus. The first and perhaps most foundational component of dialectical preaching is the proposition. It is the "sermon in a sentence" in which the preacher has distilled and clarified the essential idea of the sermon, so that the message does not drift. It is the GPS (global positioning satellite) for the sermon. Once the preacher, guided by the Holy Spirit, has entered the destination address, the GPS reroutes the sermon from extraneous or incorrect paths and keeps the journey focused. The proposition can also be likened to a guardrail which guides the message back onto the track laid out by the preacher in planning the sermon. This guardrail is also a guarantor of integrity and originality. If the preacher begins and sticks with an organizing idea that she or he has birthed, the likelihood is greater that the sermon will reflect a suitable level of originality throughout.

Subjects for sermons are too often overlooked as a vital aspect of construction. The subject is another name for the title of the sermon. Subjects are like fitted sheets. They must cover the entire bed but not hang loosely off at the edges. The subject must cover ideologically the entirety of the sermon; that is, the subject as stated must have relevance, on its face, to every part of the sermon, from beginning to end. The Subject must relate to, capsulize, and summarize the proposition and every other component of the sermon.

Whether the introduction of the sermon is predominantly framed by the thesis or the antithesis, the characteristics of introductions in other sermon structures should still pertain. The introduction of a sermon must set the tone. Its first assignment is to grab the listeners' attention, either with the element of surprise or with content which, on the basis of the preacher's exegesis of the congregation, she or he has determined will be of some interest to the listeners. Miles Jones has described the introduction of a sermon as the front porch of a shotgun house. One can shoot a shotgun standing on the front porch through the open front door, pass through every room of the house and hit nothing as the bullet passes from the front door out through the back door. The construction of a sermon should have a similar property; it should have simplicity, continuity, and functional flow. Functionally, Jones was suggesting that in a sermon, just as in a shotgun house, one "room" or part of the construction leads simply and seamlessly to another. The front porch, or the introduction, provides the necessary preamble to the various rooms of the house, or the other elements of the sermon, which are to be laid out as the sermon develops.

Be prudent with regard to the length of introductions. There is no recipe; this is one aspect of the "art of the preparation and delivery of sermons."[6] Too many sermons fail and listeners lose interest by the time the introduction is over, either because it was too long or the content of it was too uninteresting to the congregation. In dialectical preaching, the introduction can consist of either the thesis or the antithesis. The preacher must use discretion as to which would provide the most illuminating presentation of the material at hand. In either case, the introduction's length must be penultimate, and not overbearing.

The thesis, or the ideal, which often serves as the introduction to the dialectical sermon, is that component which outlines what the world would look like if God's desired outcome for the condition of existence addressed by the sermon existed. The thesis must paint the picture, it must establish the parameters of the way things ought to look, or ought to work out, if the mitigating factors which occasioned this sermon did not exist. In the case of a eulogy or funeral sermon, it may be advisable for the thesis to be considerably shorter than the antithesis, because thoroughly outlining the "problem" (as the antithesis will soon do) is what facilitates resolution of it later on.

The sermon example in chapter 6 provides a good example of how the thesis paints the picture of the ideal or desired condition of existence. In that sermon, the thesis establishes prayer as the antidote to the poison of grief. In this and many cases when the thesis serves as introduction to the sermon, it becomes almost a 'straw man' which is knocked down by the antithesis. The thesis is eventually reestablished as not only the desired end, but the norm when the relevant question is raised and answered in the body of the sermon, which is called the synthesis. (See below for more on *antithesis, relevant question,* and *synthesis*.)

The antithesis, or the real, outlines in contrast why the world does not resemble the ideal that the thesis has developed. The antithesis lifts up in high relief the irritants in the lives of listeners which give occasion for an answer from the text under review. The antithesis is not necessarily negative but must always be problematic. It must not veer into being fatalistic but must instead be bluntly realistic in order for its impact to be properly felt. The antithesis is the area of the sermon in which the fears, anxieties, deficiencies, or other struggles of the congregation cathartically collide with the truth of Scripture. This creates a crisis of a sort, which can be addressed only by the relevant question which is to follow.

If the thesis can be likened to the warm water of idealism and the antithesis to the cold water of reality, the relevant question is the crosscurrent, the consternation created when these two opposites collide. The relevant question is a turbulence which must be calmed. It cannot be allowed to continue swirling because its urgency is such that anyone caught in its undertow will feel a necessity for an answer to it. The preacher must ensure that this question is no mere static, semantic query. It must be sufficiently universal in its applicability that every person in the room will want to know its answer. Remember, hearers have, by definition, come to a funeral with profound and troubling questions stemming from their grief. This question is a prime opportunity to provide clarity and sometimes resolution to these deep questions of life and death.

The answer to the relevant question is pronounced in the synthesis. The synthesis amounts to the points or moves of the sermon.[7] Each point in the synthesis is in some way a part of the answer to the relevant question. The synthesis may have two or more points, and this depends upon the structure and content of the passage at hand. Discretion must be exercised here as well, because as Braxton advises, the preacher must guard against the temptation to write a eulogy or funeral sermon which attempts to do too much.[8]

I will add that it really is a worse offense to preach at a funeral a sermon which does not attempt to do enough. A eulogy or funeral sermon is guilty of not doing enough when it fails to connect the hearers to the Good News of the Gospel. Preaching at a funeral is not actually Christian preaching at all if it is simply a maudlin re-telling of the life of the deceased. There must be a connection to biblical themes and the redemptive love and power of God through Jesus Christ. Without this, the message may be a speech, it may even be an elegy, but it is definitely not a sermon. A delicate balance must be struck and must be informed by the preacher's knowledge of the congregation, the milieu and conduct of the worship service, the text at hand, and the preacher's skill in organizing and managing the message.

At this point in the conclusion or celebration of the sermon in African American contexts, it may be effective to use a quotation from a familiar song which is appropriate for the occasion. Sermon celebrations may call for more extended quotations, but the length of the quotation depends upon the milieu of the service once the celebration begins. (For more about celebration, see the section "The Agony and the Irony: A Word about Celebration in Preaching.")

## Other Expository Forms

Expository preaching, according to Henry Mitchell, is a simple, straightforward, verse-by-verse unearthing of the meaning of a given text and may cover a panoply of ideas and issues. Its scope of work is determined by the structure and length of the text in question, and it does not go into great depth on any given verse. According to James Earl Massey, expositional preaching focuses deeply on one main idea of a given passage.[9]

Haddon Robinson defines expository preaching as "the communication of a biblical concept, derived from and transmitted through a historical, grammatical, and literary study of a passage in its context, which the Holy Spirit first applies to the personality and experience of the preacher, then, through the preacher, applies to the hearers."[10] (See chapters 9 and 10 for examples.)

When submitting his contribution to this book, Brad Braxton, author of the sermon in chapter 9, commented on the expository genre in this way:

> In expository preaching, as in other forms of preaching, images speak to the rational mind and to the feeling heart. Discussing a "homiletics of imagery," Richard Eslinger remarks, "Much more than serving to ornament cognitive thinking, images perform an essential function in the human process of knowing—and feeling."[11] A homiletics of imagery aims not to prove a point but rather to prompt an experience. Jennifer Lord insists that imagery "is the type of language we reach for because we know the 'magnitude and particularity of the subject defy description.'"[12] The enormity of death and eternal life exhaust the capacity of informational prose. To move hearts and minds through the valley of the shadow of death to new heights of hope, our words must soar on the wings of poetic imagery.

## Application Method[13]

Funeral sermons constructed using the application method are designed to connect the experience of the listener with the biblical text (see chapter 7 for an example). The method utilizes an engagement of life events through a series of questions and a system of analysis. It begins with a personal reflection from the preacher. In this personal perspective, and in all subsequent parts of the sermon, the preacher attempts to develop a new and hopeful way of viewing life from the preacher's perspective (based on the scriptural text). The system of analysis employed in the application method looks deeply into and wrestles biblically with some struggle of the hearer in the context of death, and seeks to reframe either the thinking or responses to life of those who mourn.

This method is well suited to the busy preacher who may need to preach impromptu or who may be looking for a model simple and straightforward enough to ward off the temptation to pull out a Saturday night special (a sermon thrown together late on

Saturday night). In the case of a funeral sermon or eulogy, the application method is a good tool for moving the biblical discussion to the more intimate level where every grieving person can have personal issues addressed and can aspire to some personal behavioral ideal.

The necessity of preparing for a funeral almost always intrudes into an already overextended schedule, so effectively preaching from outlines is a valuable skill. The preacher often has to glean personal details about the deceased from bits of printed matter and brief overheard conversations. The preacher must also balance the pastoral duty to show some level of intimate concern for the unknown deceased with the theological imperative to preach Good News to the living. (See chapter 8 for an example of a funeral sermon emerging from a circumstance where the preacher had no prior knowledge of the deceased or her family.)

## The Inductive Method

It may be that the most effective structure or method for preaching at funerals is the inductive method (see chapters 11, 12, and 13). Inductive preaching allows the listener to arrive, as if conducting an investigation, at whatever conclusions the sermon holds toward the end of the message rather than at the beginning. Inductive structure does not state a premise and then set about building a case for it. As a type of narrative sermon, inductive preaching builds a case through telling a story and gradually allows the listener to see the big picture. It proceeds from observation to interpretation. Think in terms of Sherlock Holmes: "Elementary, my dear Watson!"

The life of a person who has died lends itself to weaving a yarn, to telling a story which progressively unwinds in the same way that a simple story does. Fred Craddock argues that the sermon ought to move like a good story, because stories are the best vehicles for what he has called "indirect speech" and "Overhearing the Gospel."[14] Indirect speech allows listeners to draw their own conclusions rather than to have the preacher prescriptively and dogmatically direct the content that is received. Indirect speech makes a point by allowing listeners to unearth it from within the development of a story (see chapter 13). Hearers are much more likely to receive with a sense of wonder that which they discover themselves.

Further, listeners are engaged by inductive preaching in a fascinating exercise in biblical eavesdropping. By utilizing this method, the preacher, like a docent in a museum, takes the listeners on a guided tour of biblical content. To extend the metaphor, the preacher does not force listeners to view an exhibit; she or he approaches the exhibit with the listeners and introduces it. When done well, this form facilitates "Aha!" moments between the hearers and the text. Before listeners know it, by the unfolding of a story they have been introduced to some biblical insight or perspective which sheds light on the life of the deceased or shines some light on the meaning of biblical content. In a sense, the hearers have been "listening at the door" of biblical truth.

Every good inductive sermon follows a few simple rules. First, inductive preaching is textual. It can be argued that narrative and inductive preaching by definition are topical because they deal with a story which always includes a point, but inductive preaching should always be anchored in a biblical text rather than a mere topic. The obvious purpose of anchoring in a text is to keep the focus of the message on biblical transformation and not allow the hearers to become disabled by grief or the preacher to be detoured by too much thematic axe grinding.

Second, inductive preaching assists hearers in drawing connections between the text and the story. This can be accomplished by utilizing transitional phrases, word pictures, or even quotations from songs or other writers. In the case of funeral preaching, many times the story being told is the life story, or some aspect of it, of the deceased.

Third, inductive sermons are amorphous in terms of structure. Because they are shaped by the content and flow of the biblical text and by the content and flow of the life of the deceased, every inductive sermon has its own structure. Inductive sermons are not likely to have three neat points of exposition and a poem at the end.

## The Agony and the Irony: A Word about Celebration in Preaching

In preaching, the term "celebration" deals with the notion of concluding the sermon. In the African American context, parenthetic to the conclusion is moving the hearers to a concrete response to the preaching. Frank Thomas, in *They Like to Never Quit Praisin' God: The Role of Celebration in Preaching*, provides an extended quotation from an interview with a former slave, Ned Walker, who recounts almost verbatim his experience hearing a slave preacher deliver a eulogy. Thomas uses the story to illustrate the operational purpose of celebration in the sermon. The distillation of the matter is that when the people in the funeral service came face to face with the grace of God as preached, they responded.[15]

The point is, whether the response is praise, a change of heart or mind, or even action outside of the sanctuary, the objective is the same: move hearers to respond. Just what type of response is elicited depends upon the objective of the sermon. For funerals, the chief objective for preaching must at least be to begin the process of transformation from grief to recovery. How this is accomplished is a matter of specific concern.

Celebration is characterized by several identifying markers. First, it must always be connected rhetorically to the body of the sermon and not tacked on at the end for effect. The celebration must recapitulate the main points of the sermon, and if it is done well, it will also at least theologically reiterate the organizing principle, or proposition (see page 51). Celebrations are more like journeys than they are destinations. Celebration is a gradual progression toward the conclusion of the whole matter. Ideally the celebration is even connected to the title of the sermon by a gossamer thread of kerygmatic content. One cannot simply holler "Jesus" at the end of the message and expect celebration to have been properly carried out. It is also unacceptable to assume the old stand-by position of recounting the crucifixion and the resurrection, as moving as that story always is, and expect that the celebration box has been checked off on the "List of Things to Do While Celebrating."

Second, the preacher must decide at the outset of the sermon what behavioral response this sermon requires. This is accomplished by deciding whether the existential problem first teased out and then addressed by the sermon is a problem of the mind, the heart, or the soul. If the sermon addresses a matter of the mind, then the celebration must be a thinking conclusion. If it addresses a problem of the heart, the celebration must center around feeling or doing. If the sermon addresses a matter of the soul, then the celebration must be a conclusion centered around deciding; specifically, deciding to make a discipleship commitment. The preacher wants the hearers to think, feel or do, or decide. Whichever action is desired, the preacher as the result of the celebration always wants the hearers to do something.[16]

It is assumed that every faithful preacher approaches the task wearing the heavy yoke of a scholar. No preacher is fit or able to stand tall behind the sacred desk without first having bowed low before the burning bush. With this in mind, it is here that I digress from the traditional rhetorical methods of many homilists and teachers of homiletics. The term "celebration" is referred to as such, as opposed to the term "conclusion," in an effort to highlight the transformative assignment which is at the heart of the task. A conclusion is more indicative of something the preacher as rhetorician and tactician does for people. The celebration is indicative of something the preacher does as liturgist in the midst of the people. Both tasks are inherently scholarly enterprises.

One task, however, is also primarily spiritual. This liturgical collaboration between preacher and people is the power by which the Holy Spirit begins to consummate the ultimate preaching assignment: incarnation and transformation. Celebration occurs when the hearers in the congregation, together with the preacher, arrive at the realization that God has supernaturally spoken in the Word and through the preacher. When engaged with integrity, the moment of celebration in black preaching can be a tremendously powerful process.

If the preacher has studied adequately, there are always more clippings on the cutting-room floor than she or he will ever have ample time to preach in one sermon. It is these clippings, along with the reflections on the preacher's experience and existential realities within the congregation, which can provide the fodder for celebration. Conventional wisdom also requires that celebrations not introduce new material into the sermon. Recapitulation is key; however, scraps from the cutting-room floor are in order here as long as they serve the purpose of advancing the behavioral response. Celebration can be written or extemporaneous, but it must always be a work of spiritual creativity drawn from the context of ecclesial tradition, the social location of the community,[17] and the authentic being of the preacher. It must also conform to the traditional identifying homiletic markers and must, therefore, ultimately promote a cogent, coherent conclusion to the sermon.

When I teach preaching, I liken this moment to a preacher approaching the precipice of a cliff. Opposite the cliff is another cliff, but that cliff is much farther away than the preacher can reach by jumping. Separating the two cliffs is a deep ravine, so deep that the bottom can scarcely be seen. During the celebration, it is the preacher's assignment to move from one cliff to another, but the only way to make the trip is to fly. Not having wings, the preacher must rely on the wind of the Holy Spirit to carry her or him to the other side. Positioning herself or himself in the wind, the preacher must stretch out, lean forward, and jump. If the preacher is not in the wind, a plummet to certain death will be the result. If, however, the preacher has leaped onto the wind, the Holy Spirit will carry the preacher, via the Spirit's own route, to the other side. Along the way, the Spirit will instruct the preacher to pick up from the cutting-room floor certain scraps left behind during the inspiration of study, scraps which perhaps were strategically omitted from the body of the sermon. These will be just the pieces that those in the audience will need to elicit their call to action. The preacher will not know which people need which pieces, but the Spirit, who charts the course through pathless air across the ravine to the other side, knows.

Contrary to the specious observations of some outside the tradition and some inside as well, celebration in preaching is not emotional self-indulgence, or at least it should not be. Some celebration has been commandeered by preaching imposters and others commonly called jacklegs, charlatans who prey on the ignorance and emotions of people and who, through their own ignorance and lazy scholarship, do violence to the pulpit and the people. In celebration, the Spirit must be sovereign over the intellect and the emotions. Moreover, intellect and emotion are not mutually exclusive. As John Kinney says, "Thinking people ought to shout, and shouting people ought to think."[18]

This experience is what infuses black preaching with its unique cultural cadence and artfully ingenious rhetoric, and it is what elicits the call and response which has so characterized black worship over the years. This celebration experience is what caused the mourners at Uncle Wash's funeral in 1866 to experience a change of thinking and break out in a shout such that "they like to never quit praisin' God!"[19]

## NOTES

1. Paul Tillich, *Biblical Religion and the Search for Ultimate Reality* (Chicago: University of Chicago Press, 1955), 33.

2. Brad Braxton, "Farewell to My Father: Reflections from a 'Preacher's Kid,'" available at http://www.theafricanamericanlectionary.org/preachingHome.asp, 6–8, 2010 (accessed February 17, 2011).

3. Samuel DeWitt Proctor, *The Certain Sound of the Trumpet: Crafting a Sermon of Authority* (Valley Forge, PA: Judson Press, 1994). Proctor did not develop the dialectical process—philosopher G. W. F. Hegel (1770–1831) did—but Proctor did pioneer the use of this method in sermon preparation. Proctor's application of the process moves the sermon deductively from the actual to the absolute, or ideal. Alternately, if the preacher chooses to position the thesis before the antithesis, the sermon moves from the ideal, or absolute, to the actual. According to Proctor, this is a matter of the preacher's choice.

4. Proctor, *Certain Sound of the Trumpet*, 53–57.

5. Ibid.

6. A definition of homiletics by Miles Jones. It can be said, however, that there is as much science to homiletics as there is art. Homiletics is comprised of specific categories, techniques, and skills. Homiletics has an esoteric method (science) which must be appropriated with competence in order for a preacher to obtain any level of mastery in its art.

7. A point or move in a sermon should ideally have two sides to one coin. On one side is the condition of existence addressed by the text. This is the biblical setting, the narrative flow, the exegetical content of the passage. On the other side is the existential relevance of the text or an answer to the question, "How does this passage address the condition of existence at hand?"

8. Braxton, "Farewell to My Father: Reflections from a 'Preacher's Kid.'"

9. See James Earl Massey in Henry H. Mitchell, *Black Preaching: The Recovery of a Powerful Art* (Nashville: Abingdon, 1990), 118. Mitchell details how Massey differentiates expository preaching from expositional preaching.

10. Haddon W. Robinson, *Biblical Preaching: The Development and Delivery of Expository Messages*, 2nd ed. (Grand Rapids: Baker Academic, 2001), 19.

11. Richard L. Eslinger, *The Web of Preaching: New Options in Homiletic Method* (Nashville: Abingdon, 2002), 251.

12. Jennifer L. Lord, *Finding Language and Imagery: Words for Holy Speech* (Minneapolis: Fortress, 2010), 13–14.

13. Rev. Nathan Dell, a distinguished retired Presbyterian pastor and teacher of homiletics at the Samuel DeWitt Proctor School of Theology in Richmond, Virginia, is a much sought-after proponent and teacher of this style.

14. Charles Campbell, *Preaching Jesus: New Directions for Homiletics in Hans Frei's Postliberal Theology* (Grand Rapids: Eerdmans, 1997), 120. Campbell cites Fred Craddock, who argues that narrative, inductive preaching is an excellent method for engaging hearers in the biblical text which is itself a story. This style represents a turn away from more rationalistic, theological, and content-oriented sermons to sermons which more easily connect the experience of the listener to the message of the Bible.

15. Frank Thomas, *They Like to Never Quit Praisin' God: The Role of Celebration in Preaching* (Cleveland: United Church Press, 1997), 31.

16. Katie Cannon, *Teaching Preaching: Isaac Rufus Clark and Black Sacred Rhetoric* (New York: Continuum, 2007), 161–62.

17. Social location is a term laden with theological significance. It encompasses the totality of a person: race, gender, economic status, culture, education, geography, and spiritual qualities. Its relevance to preaching is that it defines the posture or predisposition of an individual to receive the preached Word. It identifies possible barriers or at least the filters through which a person is liable to process preaching.

18. Dr. John W. Kinney is dean of the Samuel DeWitt Proctor School of Theology at Virginia Union University in Richmond, Virginia.

19. Thomas, *They Like to Never Quit Praisin' God*, 31. According to Thomas, there was concern in the community about the fact that Uncle Wash had been to jail, causing some to wonder whether he made it into heaven. Moreover, they seemed to have been concerned whether or not any church member who had led a blemished life could be heaven-bound. Uncle Pompey, the slave preacher, clearly had as his objective to alter the thinking of the people concerning this. Thomas tells the story of how effectively and vividly the slave preacher used language in the celebration of the eulogy in order to incite change in the thinking of the community. By their response, he evidently succeeded.

▪ PART TWO ▪

# Funeral Sermons and Eulogies

▪ CHAPTER 6 ▪

# An Illness Not unto Death

## A Eulogy for Mary Frances Turner

PETER M. WHERRY

JOHN 11:1-45

*Now a certain man was ill, Lazarus of Bethany, the village of Mary and her sister Martha. It was Mary who anointed the Lord with ointment and wiped his feet with her hair, whose brother Lazarus was ill. So the sisters sent to him, saying, "Lord, he whom you love is ill." But when Jesus heard it he said, "This illness is not unto death; it is for the glory of God, so that the Son of God may be glorified by means of it."* (John 11:1-4 RSV)

The eulogy which follows was preached on the occasion of the death of one of our family's dearest friends. Mary Frances Turner[1] was not only godmother to our adult son, Justin, but we are godparents to her adult daughter, Faith. We shared almost thirty-two years of friendship much like brothers and sisters. Frannie's death was one of those instances in which many questions of faith arose, because so much prayer had been lifted for her and a prophecy about her healing had been spoken. The prophecy was problematic, at least to my wife and me, because I was used to deliver the message to Frannie's daughter, and we saw Frannie recover briefly following the laying on of hands as the result of the prophecy. I chose to frame the eulogy as a dialectical sermon because I find that type to be particularly useful in dissecting and wrestling with difficult or controversial issues of doctrine, faith, or experience. This was surely an occasion for wrestling with difficult issues.

Proposition: The death of a loved one is, for the believer, an invitation to faith, not despair.

Subject: "An Illness Not unto Death"

Text: John 11:1-45 (especially vv. 1-4): "But when Jesus heard it he said, 'This illness is not unto death; it is for the glory of God, so that the Son of God may be glorified by means of it.'"

## Introduction (Thesis):

WORD OF FRANNIE'S ILLNESS reached us on Thursday, the night after the fateful surgery during which the physicians emerged from the operating room, unable to complete it because her condition was so grave. News that someone we love is ill and near death is always a shock, and this news was every bit a punch in the gut.

We, as the people of God, are always challenged to have faith during these pressing times, and we work hard to grow up into the rangy armor of our confession. We immediately go into prayer, and this is what we should do. We have learned from hard experience that prayer does, indeed, change things. We are, after all, the heirs of the legacy of James, who admonished the church of Jerusalem that if any are sick, let them call upon the elders of the church, so that they may anoint them with oil, pray over and lay hands on them, and James assures us, the sick shall recover.[2]

Prayer during these times of crisis becomes a reflex. Through prayer, we can stare grim reality right in the face and see recovery. This is not denial of the facts on the ground, but it is instead a glimmering glimpse of otherworldly reality. Reaching out for Jesus through prayer is

> the soul's sincere desire,
> Unuttered or expressed;
> The motion of a hidden fire
> That trembles in the breast.[3]

## Transition (Antithesis):

There are times, however, when it seems that even heaven conspires to extinguish the hidden watch fires of prayer. There are moments on the journey with a loved one through valleys of illness that prayer begins to feel like a feeble last resort. Oh, I know we believers are loath to admit it. We fear that someone may just revoke our "disciple's card" if we ever admit to encountering moments of doubt or fear or failure or futility when someone we love is dying.

If you have ever experienced any of those feelings, it is easier to understand how the sisters of Lazarus must have felt when they sent word to Jesus that their brother, Lazarus, was sick. This message was delivered in such a way that it was fairly clear he had no mere head cold, but in spite of the gravity of the news, Jesus didn't rush to Bethany, where they lived. The text conveys that he did not go for two more days. Instead, Jesus utters what for any of us who have watched Frannie's departure are some very disturbing words. In verse 4, he says, "This illness is not unto death."

I was disturbed when I reread these words during the week, and I feel certain that many in this room today have been disturbed by them at some point in this journey. The words are disturbing because they are clearly counterintuitive; they contradict the subsequent reality. By the time Jesus got to Bethany, his friend, Lazarus, *had* died. The words are disturbing because they are followed by a statement explaining that the illness "is for the glory of God, so that the Son of God may be glorified by means of it."

These words are troubling because they may sound glib, almost callous to the casual hearer. They almost seem to suggest that Jesus is unfazed by the obvious suffering of his friend and the understandable anxiety of his friend's two sisters. The words, on their face, seem to betray his willingness to use this occasion for some unspoken advantage of his own. As he usually does in this Gospel, John has laced this story with dual meanings. The physical death of Lazarus is just a fact. He does die. Every one of us who went in and out of that hospital with Frannie found ourselves feeling incredulous: "I just can't believe I am doing this! Not Frannie. Not now. She's always been so full of life, so full of fun, so strong and present for everyone else."

My mind is so full of memories of meals at the Turners' dinner table where Mrs. Mamie Turner, Frannie's mom, would challenge everybody, especially me, "Clean it up," meaning, "Eat everything I put on the table." There would be Frannie, laughing and helping her dad and us to "sop the gravy" with Mrs. Turner's exquisite homemade rolls.

Who could forget how Frannie loved her precious daughter, Faith, and now Faith's marvelous family, her husband, James, and their children, Trey, Jordan, and Jeremiah. Faith was the apple of her mother's eye. She was the pinnacle of womanhood and success in the world that Frannie didn't have the chance to achieve for herself because she was such a sacrificial and faithful mother.

Memories abound of family times with Frannie's siblings, Junior and his wife Jen, Gertrude and Lloyd, my wife Wanda and me, and all the "Turner" children. Frannie seemed so often to be the glue that drew us all together.

How many times have we sat at the conference table with Frannie at the old BGC[4] office building, planning this event or the other? How many times have we keeled over laughing with Frannie as she would get burned out by the complicated and always controversial ticket sales for the meal functions at the annual session? On one of those hilarious occasions, my wife, Wanda, who was assisting Frannie with the events that year, mentioned tickets to Frannie for one of the meal functions, and Frannie was so tired of handling tickets that she looked at us with wild eyes, tilted her head like a woman gone crazy, and asked in a high-pitched voice, "Tickets?! You want tickets?!" and proceeded to throw the tickets up into the air like confetti, and all over the bed of her hotel room.

Most of you in this room, especially her close and lifelong friends like Ronald and Ailene, Jimmy and Teresa, the gang from Sixth Baptist,[5] Mrs. Ella Grimes, and Mrs. Catherine James—all of you can recall hours of hilarious, sometimes nefarious capers you enjoyed with Frannie.

The community is also full of scores, hundreds of people whom Frannie's generous heart touched. She was a bucket of water when it came to the pain of others and would do anything for even a stranger. She mentored and mothered countless college students like Gloria and Paula, Mary and Barry, Wanda and me, and seminarians galore! As many of us whom I have just named stood at her bedside, we found ourselves wondering, "Now, can it be that I am here saying good-bye to her? It just can't be." But it was. She was sick, gravely sick. Making matters even more complicated, she did die.

The reason her death is a complication is that so much prayer went up for her during those weeks of her illness, and especially at the last, that if we're honest, critical questions of faith are teased to the surface. Does her death mean that God did not answer the prayers I know were raised on her behalf? Does it mean that prayers for healing just did not work this time? Does it mean that all of our rejoicing during the brief moments of recovery was foolish and presumptuous? Does it mean that the words spoken during her illness about her recovery were false prophecy? We prayed, but she did die. We had faith, but she died anyway.

But like everything else in this story, and in the story of Frannie's life, there is a dual dimension. Real peace and power will come only to those of us who can keep up with both story lines.

*Relevant Question*: How is it possible for a death so painful and in such seeming defiance of our faith to lead us to faith?

## Synthesis 1: We must understand the mission of Jesus.

> Thus he spoke, and then he said to them, "Our friend Lazarus has fallen asleep, but I go to awake him out of sleep." (John 11:11 RSV)

The answer comes as the story of Jesus attending to the death of his dear friend unfolds. The dynamics of death are painful to us because they are usually at odds with our own vision of the world. We perceive at times of illness and death that it is the mission of Jesus to heal, and if death occurs, we over-spiritualize the matter and declare, "It was his will."

But when Jesus was explaining his plans to go to Bethany for Lazarus, he made it clear that he was not going to attend a funeral. That's why he didn't bother to run down as soon as he got the news. Jesus made it clear that his friend Lazarus was sleeping, and it was his expressed mission to go and wake him up (v. 11).

We will find faith when we realize that, as crucial hours come and it seems that our desires are at odds with the facts on the ground, Jesus makes his way to us, in his perfect time, to turn out a slumber party. His agenda is to redefine death, not to acquiesce to it. His agenda is to reimage the funeral, not to become a mourner in the midst.

*Relevant Question*: How is it possible for a death so painful and in such seeming defiance of our faith to lead us to faith?

## Synthesis 2: We must understand the method of Jesus.

> Bethany was near Jerusalem, about two miles off, and many of the Jews had come to Martha and Mary to console them concerning their brother. (John 11:18-19 RSV)

Jesus is palpably close to meeting his own date with destiny on the cross, and this episode of his ministry clearly inflames the ire of his enemies. Bethany's proximity to Jerusalem, the holy city, sets an ominous backdrop for this story to unfold. Looming over the graveyard where Jesus stood and wept with his dear friends is Jerusalem, the place where Jesus will surrender and die.

Moreover, the nineteenth verse adds another ominous tinge to the story. Many Jews had come to mourn with Martha and Mary. These Jews would be the antagonists for the trumped-up charges by which Jesus would die.

This is the method of Jesus. He chooses to redefine death in the very shadow of death-dealing reality. This is an invitation to faith: to know that this same Jesus who has passed through the cruel crucible of suffering stands with us where suffering, pain, illness, and death cast an ominous chill.

He is not absent. He is not divorced from our plight. He has come fearlessly alongside us to reimage brutality and death. Now, because of him, hospitals can become hotels where weary souls find rest. Now, because of him, one can be sick and yet live well. Now, because of him, we are never alone in our seasons of distress and grief. Now, because of him, the lonely, barren, frightful, unintelligible places of life become gardens where Jesus is waiting. Somebody said, "He walks with me, and he talks with me, and he tells me I am his own."[6]

*Relevant Question*: How is it possible for a death so painful and in such seeming defiance of our faith to lead us to faith?

# Synthesis 3: We must understand the mind of Jesus.

> Jesus said to her, "I am the resurrection and the life; he who believes in me, though he die, yet shall he live, and whoever lives and believes in me shall never die. Do you believe this?" (John 11:25-26 RSV)

Chapters 1 through 12 of this Gospel are called the Book of Signs. This story about the raising of Lazarus is the seventh and final episode in that section. All of the signs point to God, and they are constructed in a way that can be understood only through the eyes of faith. Moreover, these words of Jesus are one of the several *ego eime*, or "I am," sayings of Jesus in John.

When someone who looms so large and who has been such an integral part of life, as Frannie has, departs from us, it can be challenging to find faith in the midst of our grief. But here, Jesus challenges us to understand his mission: to redefine death not as a ditch but as a doorway. We can find faith when we understand his method. He chooses to redefine death and the death-dealing circumstances it brings by coming to us right in the shadow of our struggle. He is a very present help in time of trouble. His method is incarnated love.

But we will truly find faith when we understand the mind of Jesus. There is an old saying that if someone tells you who they are, believe them. There is no better way to discern just what the mind of Jesus is concerning the pain that we feel today than to hear his own thinking about himself.

Now this is crucial, because unless you understand the mind of Jesus, you may just be overwhelmed by grief, or worse, gripped by fear. This is because Frannie's death came in spite of a prophecy spoken by an old man about her. Wanda and I traveled to Savannah, Georgia, where I was to lecture for the National Baptist Convention's Eastern Region Board. While there, I looked up my late mother's former pastor, Rev. Henry R. Delaney, a C.M.E.[7] pastor of many years. He is a very old man now, confined to a wheelchair, and we found him slumped in an oversized recliner in his den. I had not seen him since 1966, and he was no baby, even then.

After nearly an hour of pleasantries and catching-up conversation, he described to us an episode of charismatic power which he encountered in 1984. He was asked to pray for a lady during a revival he was invited to preach, and to his amazement, as he prayed, he saw people falling out all around the church. Being a dyed-in-the-wool C.M.E., this was alien to him, and the elders and bishops above him taught against it and disapproved assiduously his "dabbling" in this stuff. Nonetheless, this experience continued to happen, and the result was consistently that those for whom he prayed got well.

Some time later in our conversation, as we talked about our families and prepared to leave, he stopped, virtually in mid-sentence, and announced, "There's a lady who is gravely ill, but you will lay your hands on her and she will get well." He then demonstrated how the laying on of hands was to be done and described from where on my right hand the power for the healing would come. Wanda and I looked at each other quizzically and pondered this visit most of the way home.

Little did we know at that time that Frannie would fall gravely ill. When we got to Richmond to say our good-byes to her after the surgery, Wanda asked me, "Will you lay your hands on Frannie?" I felt strongly that although I hadn't known at the time who the old prophet was describing, Frannie was the one. So when we entered her room in the ICU [intensive care unit], Wanda, our daughter, Bethany, and I joined hands to pray, and I laid my hand on her. As I did, I felt the two jolts of power that the old prophet described, and Wanda, on the other side of the bed touching Frannie's hand, felt them, too.

Following this episode, we said nothing to anyone, but when we got back to Charlotte, we called Faith and described what had happened. We lived in hope over the next day or so until Friday, when we received a call from Faith informing us that Frannie was off the respirator, sitting up a little in the bed, and the staff had begun exercising her limbs. She was placing food orders and telling people whom she wanted to cook what. We were jubilant.

Monday, we received word that on Sunday night she had taken a turn for the worse, and by Wednesday, she was gone. Now I know the let-down Martha must have felt. This experience churned up all manner of theological heartburn. Had the prophet been wrong, and we just participated in some wishful thinking? Had the whole brief recovery simply been a symptom of what we've seen many times—a last burst of strength leading up to the end? In my prayer time Monday, I heard the enemy taunting me, "See, you shouted too soon. All this talk of healing and laying on hands did nothing but get people's hopes up." But wait a minute! That is not the end of the story.

Martha had run out to meet Jesus when she heard that he was close-by. Mary stayed home with the guests and mourned. Both of them at least said that if Jesus had been there, Lazarus would still be alive. But, after four days, even the loquacious Martha cut short the notion that anything could be done now. Jesus, in an attempt to reassure her, informs her that her brother will rise again. Jesus says to her, "I know he's dead now, but 'trouble don't last always.'"[8] Martha, in turn, regurgitated the age-old theology of her forebears that he will rise again with the rest of the nation on the last day. "But," it seems Martha might say, "my heart is breaking right now!"

Isn't that just like us—quick to reject faith in favor of what look like facts because facts, according to John Adams, are stubborn things? But the Gospel writer offers her and us today a glimpse into the mind of Jesus. Jesus said to her, "Stop looking so far ahead to the resurrection that is to come. I AM the resurrection and the life. Anyone who believes in me, even though he dies, will still live, and whoever lives and believes in me, will never die." Jesus speaks this "I AM" language like Elohim at the burning bush.

In the end, this is not really about the resurrection of Lazarus. It is about the resurrection of Jesus. It's about the fact that Lazarus could get up because Jesus is himself the embodiment of resurrection power. That means the old prophet was right. She did get well. Because Jesus got up, we are here today, not to say good-bye to Frannie but to say, "See you later." Because Jesus got up, Frannie's sickness was not unto death. She could not die. Healing was the only option. She fell asleep. She blinked her eyes in an instant and woke up in eternity. She shut her eyes in corruption and opened them in incorruption. She shut her eyes in pain and confusion and opened them in peace, clarity, and glory. She heard the voice of the resurrection and the life commanding, "Loose her, and let her go." She heard him calling, "Frannie, come forth!" and on Wednesday afternoon about one o'clock in the afternoon, she came forth out of death, shook off the grave clothes of sickness and suffering, and now walks in brand-new life.

---

**NOTES**

1. This is the first of only a few instances in this book where the names of the deceased and her or his family and friends have not been changed. As is the case in other instances where actual names are used, this is done partly in tribute to the deceased and because she is well and widely known. It was my conclusion that using her name would not compromise any right to privacy, and I have secured the permission of her daughter to use this eulogy in this way.

2. James 5:14-15.

3. The first stanza of "Prayer Is the Soul's Sincere Desire" (1818), lyrics by James Montgomery (1771–1854). The lyrics were set to music by Thomas Hastings (1840), John B. Dykes (1866), Maltbie D. Babcock (1889), and Robert McCutchan (1935).

4. Baptist General Convention of Virginia. For twenty-three years, Frannie was administrative secretary to the convention's executive minister at that time, Rev. Cessar L. Scott. As is the case with many administrative secretaries, Frannie's job often included duties far beyond her pay grade, even tasks such as leading a curriculum writing team for youth retreats. Many of the listeners in the audience during her funeral worked alongside her during these times.

5. Sixth Baptist Church in Richmond, Virginia, was Frannie's church since childhood. Its pastor, Rev. Dr. Yvonne J. Bibbs, was kind enough to allow me to be the eulogist at Frannie's request.

6. A quotation from the refrain of "In the Garden" (1912), lyrics and music by C. Austin Miles (1868–1946). This gospel song is in the public domain.

7. Christian Methodist Episcopal.

8. Taken from an African American folk song in the public domain. The date and composer of this song are unknown.

· CHAPTER 7 ·

# Blessings beyond Burial

## Funeral Sermon for Orlando Morris Norris

NATHAN DELL
GENESIS 25:7-11

*These are all the years of Abraham's life that he lived, one hundred and seventy-five years. Abraham breathed his last and died in a ripe old age, an old man and satisfied with life; and he was gathered to his people. Then his sons Isaac and Ishmael buried him in the cave of Machpelah, in the field of Ephron the son of Zohar the Hittite, facing Mamre, the field which Abraham purchased from the sons of Heth; there Abraham was buried with Sarah his wife. It came about after the death of Abraham, that God blessed his son Isaac.* (Genesis 25:7-11 NASB)

The application method[1] sermon that follows is a full manuscript by Nathan Dell, seminary homiletics instructor at the Samuel DeWitt Proctor School of Theology at Virginia Union University and revered retired Presbyterian pastor. Rev. Dell is a sought-after artisan in this method and preaches this as a funeral sermon rather than a eulogy. It is instructive that he makes no incursions into the personal life of the deceased but rather delves profoundly into the universal experiences of every person's struggles with death, with loss in general, and the loss of loved ones in particular. This is the power of the application method: it is designed to allow the hearers to make practical application of a text to the everyday issues they face in life. Rev. Dell's approach is deeply biblical, and even as he works through the matrix of the method, he takes great pains to provide practical application of the text to the lives of those who were worshipers in the service. This sermon was preached in 2002, when national and personal grief in the wake of the September 11, 2001, terrorist attacks were still fresh.

Proposition: God blesses us after the death of loved ones.
Personalized Proposition: God blesses you after the death of loved ones.
Transitional Question: What blessing does God give us after the death of loved ones?
Answers:

1. God blesses us with new friends after the death of loved ones.
2. God blesses us with delayed blessings after the death of loved ones.

Conclusion/Celebration:
In the resurrection, our bodies "will be raised through Christ" and will surely receive the ultimate blessing beyond burial . . . life eternal.

OUR NATION HAS EXPERIENCED a lot of burials over the last two years. Just within the last year the nation had to bury more than three thousand people after 9/11: firemen, policemen, office workers, emergency workers. We have buried persons from our churches and community and from the seminary family. And some of us have buried members of our immediate families. So, in one sense, we all walk away from a grave in which we had to bury somebody. This brings me to the text, Genesis 25:11, which speaks of a burial and reads as follows: "After the death of Abraham, God blessed his son Isaac."

This text seems to speak of a blessing at the wrong time, on the wrong occasion. There stands a man, Isaac, over a grave in which he has just laid his father. One might suppose that when God took Abraham's last breath, he also took Isaac's last blessing, or that when God took Isaac's father, he also took Isaac's future.

When death comes, there rarely seems to be any right time. No matter how old we are (Isaac was 75) or how old our deceased loved one is (Abraham was 175), the future always appears more bleak when a beloved voice is silenced. These feelings are natural for every human being who mourns. This is particularly true when mother or father, spouse, or some wonderful guardian dies, especially if they leave young children. For with parents gone, the children's security may seem gone. So how can such a child be blessed?

How can that surviving spouse be blessed? How can a surviving friend be blessed after such a burial? Yet, we read in the text: "And it came to pass that after the death of Abraham, God blessed his son Isaac." So here, there was a blessing beyond burial.

I see two helpful words this text sets before us as we contemplate this matter of blessings beyond burial.

The first thing we see is this: In the final analysis, our good fortune does not depend upon our earthly family (relatives) but upon our heavenly Father. "Our future does not depend upon loved ones remaining with us a little longer; but upon our God who abides with us beyond the death and burial of those loved ones." If memory serves me right, Jacob voiced a similar truth centuries after Abraham's burial. When Jacob, an old man now, was about to die, he gathered his family, his children, and his grandchildren around his bedside. Then he said this to them, "I die." Their heads lowered, and their eyes watered. Then Jacob added, "But God shall be with you, and bring you again unto the land of your fathers."[2] After the death of Abraham, God blessed Isaac his son.

Yes, sooner or later we all have to bury dear ones upon whom we have depended. But God has a blessing for us, nonetheless . . . a blessing beyond that person's burial. What kind of blessing? First, God blesses us with new friendships. The Lord gives and the Lord takes away[3]. . . parents sometimes, friends sometimes, spouses sometimes . . . but God blesses us nonetheless.

Yes, he does! Sometimes the Lord blesses us with persons who are no blood kin but who become sisters and brothers to us. After a burial, God sometimes blesses us with strangers who in their care become fathers to us. God blesses us with strangers who in their concern for us become mothers to us. I believe Jesus provides an example of what I am talking about at this point. Look at Calvary. There he hangs, bleeding and dying. And his mother stands at the foot of the cross. Shocked, saddened, and shaken with grief, Jesus realizes that when he dies, Mary's future will stretch before her in bleak desolation. After all, she would lose not only her oldest son but also her master Teacher and beloved Rabbi. But in the grace of which Jesus is so full, he made provision for Mary to be blessed after his burial. And he managed to do it through his pain. With a glance of his eyes and a nod of his head, Jesus directed Mary's attention to a man who was no biological kin to her but who was a fellow disciple. And when he had her attention, Jesus said to her, "Woman, behold thy son."[4] John's Gospel record says, "And from that hour the disciple took her unto his own home."[5]

And speaking of being without mothers and fathers, it is a fallacy to think that you and I need parents only while we are children or teenagers. It is erroneous to suppose we need a big brother or a big sister only when we are little girls and little boys. No, as long as we live, even if we get to be "old and full of years" . . . we need family. To our dying day we need some men who will treat us with a father's care. We need some women to love us with a mother's affection. We need someone to counsel us with a grandmother's or a grandfather's wisdom. If we live to be well advanced in years, we need some person to be a brother, a sister, or a friend to us.

And you and I can thank God that God provides us with such people after we have buried those who are dear to us. Consider John: he did not merely take Mary into his home, but he took Mary into his heart! Folks, when death takes some relative from us, the Lord has someone ready to take us into his or her hearts. In our pain and hurt, the Lord often points us to somebody . . . and says to us, "Behold your mother, behold your father . . . behold your son, your daughter . . . behold your friend."

Therefore, when you have to bury someone who is so dear as to be almost more than life to you . . . you need not go into the future without friend or kin. Bury your dead and continue to serve God as Isaac did. Bury your friend and continue with Job, "The LORD gave and the LORD has taken away; blessed be the name of the LORD."[6] And the Lord will bless you after the death of your loved one. While the days up ahead will seem barren and bleak, in God's mercy and in God's time, God will people those days with brothers, sisters, fathers, mothers, friends, and yes, sometimes, even with a new spouse. All praise and thanksgiving to the God who gives us blessings beyond burial, new friends and new kin. This is the first helpful word this text sets before us this morning.

I see a second word in this text which is helpful. It is this: We need to be patient as we await God's blessings beyond burial. After all, most of Isaac's blessing did not show up immediately. After he laid his father, Abraham, in his grave, the days and months dragged by, week after week, month after month, year after year. One season followed another, with years falling from the calendar like so many leaves scattered by autumn winds. In the meantime Isaac saw no further evidence of the descendants God had promised. (After being unable to conceive for the first twenty years of their marriage, Isaac and his wife, Rebekah, had only twin sons at the time of Abraham's death—and no others after that.) Even the land God had called Abraham and his offspring to inhabit was the source of more strife than blessing for Isaac at first. Indeed, at first, Isaac saw nothing of the blessings God had promised to give him. Isaac had to wait.

And this is hard to do when you must wait in the emptiness a death has caused. Waiting is hard when you must wait in a pain and loneliness which seems to affirm that God has forgotten to be gracious. It is hard to wait when it seems you won't ever again see "the goodness of the LORD in the land of the living."[7] Waiting is hard when a burial seems to have permanently denied some needed blessing. After all, if your yearning is intense, a single day without the person you long for can seem like a whole year, a year in which the tides deposit no blessings upon the shoreline of your life.

And here is where we need to be careful, lest we get tripped up. If God doesn't bless us immediately after our losses . . . if God's presence doesn't dry our eyes even before we leave the cemetery, some of us may grow impatient. If God's providence doesn't give us the material or emotional security we need right now, we may grow impatient. If sorrow's floodwaters sweep away that certainty and trust of the goodness of God we had before that death, you and I can grow impatient with the divine. When affliction's storm winds loosen your grip upon faith, a grip which once seemed so firm, we may grow impatient with God. This is one reason the psalmist writes: "Wait on the LORD; be of good courage, and he shall strengthen thine heart; wait, I say, on the LORD."[8]

Are you living in the absence of someone you dearly loved? Is it after the death of someone who was precious to you? Is it after the death of some reasonable expectation you've had to bury . . . some bright dream, some hope, some ambitious undertaking you had to leave in one of yesterday's graveyards? Is it after the death of one of these things? If so . . . bury it and wait upon God's blessing that is beyond the burial. Bury whatever and whoever is dead, and know that God is not dead! In the words of Habakkuk, "though it [the blessing] tarry, wait for it; for it will surely come" (Habakkuk 2:3 KJV).

When I began this sermon, we met Isaac standing over the grave of his father, Abraham. With Abraham dead, Isaac is alone in a hostile country. He faced many challenges in the land of promise. In fact, as soon as Isaac dug a well to furnish water for his cattle, the Philistines filled the well with dirt and stones. They wanted to deprive Isaac's cattle of the water they needed and therefore deprive Isaac of the finances those cattle would bring him.

With the death of his father, Isaac's fortune turned south; his chances for a bright, prosperous future seemed over! But was Isaac's future over? Did the death of his father deprive his future of meaning and significance? Listen to what God did for Isaac in the seasons that followed his father's death: "Now Isaac sowed in that land and reaped in the same year a hundredfold. And the LORD blessed him, and the man became rich, and continued to grow richer until he became very wealthy; for he had possessions of flocks and herds and a great household" (Genesis 26:12-14 NASB). So, in time, after the burial, Isaac received large blessings after all!

I say to you this morning, God's resources are sufficient for loss, even the loss death brings. So if you have suffered some such loss, stand over your loss, and wait on the Lord. Weep over your loss, and wait on the Lord. Pray over your loss, and wait on the Lord. Yes, your head may be waters and your eyes a fountain of tears right now; yet, in God's own good time, you will see God's salvation. Wait on the Lord. And in Christ's own way, he will bless you with what you need. He has abundant and endless resources. The Lord will dry your eyes and heal your hurt. Wait on the Lord, and beyond the burial, God will bind up your broken heart! Wait on the Lord, and beyond this burial God will comfort all who morn in Zion, to give you "a garland instead of ashes, the oil of gladness instead of mourning, the mantle of praise instead of a faint spirit."[9] Yes, there are blessings beyond burial for those who mourn in the Lord. So bury it and look ever to Jesus!

Permit me to add a postscript. Even though we are at the grave site where life has been defeated, nevertheless I see something in the gospel that can take us to the victory circle. For although God provides blessings beyond burial for the survivors, God also provides blessings beyond burial for those who are buried. Listen: "He which raised up the Lord Jesus shall raise us up also by Jesus."[10] That is the blessing beyond burial for those whom we bury! Death gave our loved one an eviction notice. Death kicked our friend out of this earthly residence. But the Lord promises our loved one a blessing beyond burial: "For we know that if the earthly house of this tabernacle were dissolved, we have a building of God, an house not made with hands, eternal in the heavens" (2 Corinthians 5:1 KJV). A blessing beyond burial awaits the buried also.

Their bodies were lowered in the grave, pitiful and perishable, weakened by age or disease, degraded and dishonored by the ravages of mortality. But in Jesus Christ, a blessing beyond burial awaits these buried bodies. Didn't Paul say it? "It is sown in corruption; it is raised in incorruption: It is sown in dishonor; it is raised in glory: it is sown in weakness; it is raised in power: It was sown a natural body; it is raised a spiritual body."[11]

In their lives, they lived in Christ. In their death, they died in Christ; and the gospel declares that in the day of resurrection, they will be raised through Christ and will surely receive the ultimate gift: blessings beyond burial . . . life eternal. "And it came to pass after the death of Abraham, that God blessed Isaac his son."

**NOTES**

1. Samuel T. Logan, Jr., editor, "Application," in *The Preacher and Preaching* (Phillipsburg, NJ: Presbyterian and Reformed, 1986), 332–333.
2. Genesis 48:21 KJV.
3. Job 1:21.
4. John 19:26 KJV.
5. John 19:27 KJV.
6. Job 1:21 NASB.
7. Psalm 27:13 KJV.
8. Psalm 27:14 KJV.
9. Isaiah 61:3 NRSV.
10. 2 Corinthians 4:14 KJV.
11. 1 Corinthians 15:42-44 KJV.

• CHAPTER 8 •

# A Lasting Fellowship

## Funeral Sermon for Beulah Jones Holder Willis

TONEY L. McNAIR JR.

1 John 1:1-4

*We write to you about the Word of life, which has existed from the very beginning. We have heard it, and we have seen it with our eyes; yes, we have seen it, and our hands have touched it. When this life became visible, we saw it; so we speak of it and tell you about the eternal life which was with the Father and was made known to us. What we have seen and heard we announce to you also, so that you will join with us in the fellowship that we have with the Father and with his Son Jesus Christ. We write this in order that our* [some manuscripts have your] *joy may be complete.* (1 John 1:1-4 GNB/TEV)

This second example of the application model by Toney L. McNair Jr. is in a modified outline form, as is customary in much funeral preaching. Toney is associate pastor for worship at the historic First Baptist Church, Bute Street, in Norfolk, Virginia. For seven and one half years, he was assistant pastor for worship and church growth while I was pastor at the historic Queen Street Baptist Church in Norfolk. Toney is skilled when it comes to Christian worship, and he is an experienced and pastoral practitioner of preaching.

As noted in chapter 5, this sermon offers a wonderful model of a message preached for the funeral of someone unknown to the preacher. The deceased in this case was not a member of the church where

Rev. Toney McNair served, but the preacher accomplishes his task effectively, preaching a funeral sermon for a person he does not know and offering compassion to a grieving family. It is also a wonderful example of the cultural nuances and structure of sermons in the African American context. Notice that the term "celebration" appears at the end of the outline and the sermon.

Proposition: God desires a lasting fellowship with those who will receive it and believe in God.

Personal Proposition: God desires a lasting fellowship with you if you will receive it and believe in God.

Transitional Question: What are the benefits of a lasting fellowship?

Answers:

1. The things you've heard (v. 1)
2. The things you've seen (v. 2)
3. The things you've experienced (vv. 1, 3)

Celebration: We can celebrate the fellowship because it makes us complete (v. 4).

*INTRODUCTION*: I WANT TO EXPRESS my condolences to Mr. Victor, the husband of the deceased; her two daughters, Toya and Monica, and their spouses; and, of course, the joy of Ms. Beulah's life: her granddaughter, Tamika. May the grace and peace of God embrace you in the oncoming days as you walk through this period in your life. Please know that the prayers of all of us are being sent so that you will never walk alone. God is here to comfort and keep you.

As I prepared myself for this moment, I asked God for guidance as to what to say to you and the friends gathered here today. He quietly instructed me to look at the obituary, and I did. I saw something fascinating that I believe will bless all of us. Read with me beginning with the paragraph "Beulah enjoyed . . .":

> Beulah enjoyed interior design shows, all kinds of flowers, staying current on the news, watching sports, basketball and football, enjoying her home and just knowing her family was happy doing whatever they were doing.
>
> One of her main joys was sitting and talking with her granddaughter, Tamika. Tamika brought her a lot of joy, light, and excitement the last years of her life. They would often lie side by side watching their favorite programs: *Clifford the Big Red Dog* and *The Barefoot*

*Contessa*. They spent a lot of time together, like two little ladies enjoying afternoon tea. Both were born in October; Tamika has taken on a lot of her grandmother's qualities.

After several readings and listening, I heard, I saw, and I experienced what was right before my very eyes: the reality of a lasting fellowship. The warm breeze of a gathering to be long remembered, the joy of laughter shared that brings a peaceful calm, the amazement of touch experienced because of love revealed—yes, fellowship. Given the fact that death has happened, there appears to be a break in this fellowship, but I would argue, "No, not really." Even more important, there can be a whole new meaning to fellowship as we consult the Lord concerning his perspective for us and this whole matter of fellowship.

In 1 John 1:1-4, we can find consolation that is relevant for such a time as this. This writing is a letter to an undesignated congregation. There are no greetings or mention of persons, places, or events in the letter. It has a twofold purpose: encouraging believers to live in fellowship with God and staying away from those who would try to destroy fellowship. It is clear and directly to the point.

*Proposition*: Essentially, God desires a lasting fellowship with those who will receive it (with you if you will receive it) and believe in him.

I am seeing some correlation here that can help us make it through this time of bereavement. I want to answer for you now a question that will reveal what God is saying to us. The question is:

*Transitional Question*: What are the benefits of a lasting fellowship?

First, the things you've heard (v. 1 [What are the benefits of the things you've heard?]).

"One of her main joys was sitting and talking with her granddaughter, Tamika." This fellowship involved listening.

John references the fact that he is speaking of having direct contact with Jesus. He was one of the first four disciples Jesus called.[1] John spoke from the reality of the many sermons, conversations, and prayers he had heard from Jesus through fellowship with him. The things that you've heard from someone you have spent time with just don't go away. The things that you've heard from someone who has reached your heart just don't go away.

Second, the things you've seen (v. 2 [What are the benefits of the things you've seen?]).

"They would often lie side by side watching their favorite programs: *Clifford the Big Red Dog* and *The Barefoot Contessa*."

John alludes to the many things that he had seen the Master do: casting out demons, turning water into wine, healing a blind man, and the list goes on.

How many things have you seen in this relationship that have meaning and substance and will last forever?

When God allows you to see some things that will impact your future, it is because he desires a lasting fellowship with you.

Finally, there are not only benefits from the things you've heard and from the things you've seen; there are benefits from the things you've experienced (vv. 1, 3 [What are the benefits of the things you've experienced?]).

"They spent a lot of time together . . . Tamika has taken on a lot of her grandmother's qualities."

John concurs that fellowship will breed oneness! He encourages a joining together in fellowship that would be even more meaningful because of one common denominator, Jesus Christ! It is a fact that when you are introduced to the Source of life, you will come to know the true meaning of why one exists. It is all because of fellowship!

Celebration[2]

---

**NOTES**

1. Mark 1:16-20.
2. The celebration, which was extemporaneous, centered around the fact that because of Jesus the fellowship which had been so sweet and cherished continues at another level after death.

▪ CHAPTER 9 ▪

# The Dividends of an Undivided Life

## Eulogy for Rev. Dr. James Allison Braxton Sr.

BRAD R. BRAXTON
MATTHEW 5:8

*"Blessed are the pure in heart, for they will see God."* (Matthew 5:8 NRSV)

The eulogy which follows, which is a powerful example of an expository sermon, was written by one of the country's most noted preachers, Brad Braxton. Brad is Lois Craddock Perkins Professor of Homiletics at Southern Methodist University in Dallas, Texas. He is also the founding senior pastor at The Open Church in Baltimore, Maryland. This eulogy was preached on the occasion of the homegoing service for Brad's father,[1] a man whom I had the privilege of meeting some years ago. Brad uses the passage from Matthew 5 to tell the story of his father's life and simultaneously does some impressive exegesis, explaining succinctly the meanings of key words and phrases in the text and opening up the biblical and contemporary contexts of the passage.

Imagery was the homiletic engine propelling the sermon. Brad makes expert use of homiletic imagery to craft three points in this sermon, describing three types of dividends that his father's well-lived life has earned: the internal, the external, and the eternal. This structure serves as the vehicle for revealing to the hearers the power and grace of the gospel message while keeping the focus on God, but also on the eloquent and joyous celebration of a life well-lived.

After nearly ten years of marriage to a finance professional, I have picked up the language of the marketplace. My wife, Lazetta, has taught me about financial assets and liabilities, account reconciliation and balance sheets. One term that she uses in her professional dealings has especially captured my attention. That term is "dividends." A dividend is an earning on an investment. A dividend is a payout that accrues from what you have paid in. A dividend is compensation for an earlier contribution.

While the term "dividend" is normally associated with the marketplace, the term applies equally as well to Jesus' Sermon on the Mount beginning in the fifth chapter of Matthew's Gospel. On a picturesque mountain in Galilee—a mountain upon which my father and I stood in May of 1997 when we visited the Holy Land together—Jesus taught a messianic seminar on the meaning of authentic discipleship. The opening section of the Sermon on the Mount consists of nine blessings that Jesus pronounces upon his followers. We refer to these as the Beatitudes, which is derived from the Latin word for "blessedness." Jesus declares that blessings come to those who commit themselves to God.

A blessing is a gift from God. A blessing is a sense of well-being because God has smiled on one's life. A blessing is a divine dividend that God grants to those who invest in righteousness.

According to Jesus, those who invest in God's kingdom receive a payout from what they have paid in. Although contributions to the kingdom are costly, the rate of return on righteous investments is excellent. Of the nine blessings that Jesus utters, one especially encapsulates the life and ministry of James Allison Braxton Sr. In Matthew 5:8, Jesus asserts, "Blessed are the pure in heart, for they will see God."

The phrase "pure in heart" aptly summarizes the journey of James Braxton. In the words of two New Testament scholars, "purity of heart [involves] . . . a singleness of intention and the desire to please God above all else."[2] You can be pure in heart and still have shortcomings. You can be pure in heart and still have stumbled and fallen a few times. The pure in heart are not morally perfect. Rather, the pure in heart are those who, in the name of God, have struggled to make their inner beliefs correspond with their outer behavior. The words "pure in heart" are biblical phraseology for integrity.

People of integrity know that the profession of one's lips and the production of one's life ought to be in harmony. In short, to be pure in heart is to have an undivided life, a life without radical moral and spiritual divisions. "Blessed are the pure in heart." Blessed are those whose moral character is undivided. Blessed are those who do not live morally fractured and phony lives. Have you ever seen morally fractured and phony people? Their personalities are so fragmented that you never know what piece of them will show up. And the piece of them they present to the public is usually not their most authentic self.

Jesus pronounces this blessing upon people struggling to be whole and holy—people who have no gaping splits in the tapestry of their testimonies. Blessed are people who live undivided lives. Blessed are those who walk what they talk. Blessed are those who are as sanctified on Monday as they are on Sunday. Blessed are those whose existence is unified and organized by a thirst for righteousness. A person with an undivided life is blessed.

James Braxton's life was undivided. He was passionately devoted to God, and his unswerving devotion to God made him eligible for divine dividends. Permit me to examine the balance sheet of my father's life and display the dividends that accrued to his account.

He has received three dividends for his undivided life. First, there is the internal dividend. Second, there is the external dividend. And finally, there is the eternal dividend.

In Matthew 5:8, Jesus employs both the present tense and the future tense. "Blessed are the pure in heart [present tense], for they will see God [future tense]." Jesus does not say that the pure in heart will be blessed. Jesus insists that the pure in heart *are* blessed—blessed in the present—blessed right now—blessed along the way. In kingdom of God compensation, there are certain dividends that disciples receive even in the present.

Thus, my father received his first dividend—an internal dividend—in the present. He daily received the dividend of being at peace with himself. There was an amazing tranquility in his inner being. There was an internal calm in him resulting from his quest for integrity. James Allison Braxton Sr. was a peaceful man. He was so peaceful because he was at peace with God. There were no vicious moral conflicts waging in his inner psyche. So many people are externally violent because they are internally divided. Not so with James Braxton. He exuded a serenity, charm, and stability that captivated the countless persons who loved him and disarmed the few persons who disliked him.

When describing Daddy to people, I often likened him to an experienced sea captain. No matter how tumultuous the wind or torrential the rain, he maintained a steady hand on the helm of the ship. He set his internal moral compass not by the sun in the sky but by the Son whom God sent to the earth.

When you have Christ in your life, you have calm in your soul. When you have calm in your soul, you are not easily irritated, nor do you fret about your obstacles and battles. Internal peace is a dividend that you, like my dad, can receive at every present moment of this pilgrimage.

Second, James Braxton received an external dividend in the present. He daily obtained the dividend of being at peace with those around him, especially his family. He possessed an undivided and uncompromised devotion to his family. His internal peace with God and with himself resulted in a marvelous external harmony with his family. For forty-four years, he was faithfully devoted to his wife, Louise, and the two of them provided an impeccable illustration of integrity for their four children. In spite of the relentless demands of his pastorate, he was a present and positive spiritual force in our home and in the wider community.

It's a blessing when your family speaks well of you. It's a blessing when the neighborhood looks up to you. It's a blessing when other pastors consider you as their pastor. It's a blessing when city officials admire you. James Braxton received the external dividend of the profound respect of those around him.

Upon learning of my father's transition to eternal life, one of my friends said to me this week, "Brad, I am not going to hell now because of your father." My father led that friend to Christ late one evening, and that friend realizes that the events of that evening altered his eternal destiny. If I were to open up this microphone to the public, undoubtedly similar testimonies would abound. So many lives, marriages, families, and careers would have been shipwrecked and doomed had it not been for the faithful and undivided living of James Braxton.

Frequently, my father would declare one of his chief axioms for living. He would assert: "I care not what you think of me. But I do care what you think of Christ because of me." Because of the godly life my father lived, so many people wanted to know, and came to know, the Christ he served.

Also, let me affirm that the external influence of my father upon our family and community would not have been possible without the constant support and strong leadership of my mother. Mama, you and Daddy transformed marital and ministerial partnership into a high art form. You, too, Louise Braxton, are the beneficiary of God's dividends. When leading a congregation, Daddy never flew solo. You were always by his side, using your considerable spiritual gifts to enhance the ministry the two of you shared. For instance, the gospel witness of First Baptist Church is so much brighter and bolder because of your contributions as well.

Many times, Mama, you had to sacrifice in the shadows and suffer in silence, but heaven has not forgotten about your struggles. God tends to have amnesia concerning our sins, but God's memory is razor sharp concerning our struggles. Heaven knows about your sacrifice, Mama, and you, too, are receiving, and will receive, dividends for your sizeable investments in the kingdom. We, your children and grandchildren, especially want to thank you for your attentive care of Daddy as he struggled with illness during the last few years. You honored the marriage vows you uttered in the summer of 1960 even when the winter of illness erupted suddenly upon your horizon. God be thanked for you, Mama.

God distributed to my father the internal dividend of inner peace and the external dividend of the respect of his family and community. For the third and final dividend—the eternal dividend—James Braxton had to await God's future. You recall that Matthew 5:8 has two verb tenses. "Blessed are the pure in heart, for they will see God." Jesus places the last half of that verse in the future tense, because we will fully apprehend God only when we enter God's future.

God's eternal future is so large that no unit of time can possibly contain it. In the present, we are constrained by hours and days, weeks and months, years and decades. These chronological limitations are absent in God's future. God's eternal future is so glorious that our corruptible bodily existence is unworthy of it. In the present, we are constrained by the imperfections and decay of our bodies. But in God's future, we are outfitted with a transformed existence. We exchange the tattered robes of our mortality for glorious garments that have embossed on them the words, "Redeemed, redeemed! My soul has been redeemed!"[3]

On August 3, 2004, James Braxton stepped into God's future and thereby became eligible to truly and fully see God. The eternal dividend of an undivided life is the privilege of being completely in God's presence. "Blessed are the pure in heart, for they will see God!" Throughout his ministry, Daddy preached about heaven, taught about heaven, and prayed for others as they made their pilgrimage into heaven. Now, hallelujah, he gets to see heaven for himself!

There's so much for him to see and do in God's future. There are jasper walls, glimmering gates, and glistening streets. There's the tree of life that has fruit to eat and leaves for the healing of life's ailments. There's the cherished reunion with his grandparents, parents, in-laws, and siblings. He can shake hands with the prophets, talk theology with the apostles, and share stories with saints like Mariah Taylor, Herbert Wiley, Minor and Hattie Wingo, those matriarchs and patriarchs of this congregation who faithfully supported his ministry.

In spite of all there is to see and do in God's future, I am persuaded that James Allison Braxton Sr. will spend the first eons of eternity simply gazing upon the glorious presence of God. He loved his wife. He loved his children, grandchildren, and extended family. He loved the church. But more than anything, Daddy loved God—the God who created him; the God who saved him; the God who commissioned him; the God who sustained him; and the God who called him to receive his eternal dividend.

Daddy used to sing that hymn, "O I want to see him."[4] Now, he sings eternally, "Yes, I can see God." Cares all past . . . home at last. Congratulations, Daddy! Cares all past . . . home at last. We celebrate your freedom, Daddy. Cares all past, home at last . . . ever to rejoice!

"Blessed are the pure in heart, for they will see God." Blessed is James Allison Braxton Sr., for now he sees God forever and ever, Amen.

## NOTES

1. Because the deceased is Brad's father, none of the names in this sermon have been changed.

2. W. D. Davies and Dale C. Allison Jr., *The Gospel According to Saint Matthew*, vol. 1 (Edinburgh: T & T Clark, 1988), 456.

3. This quotation is from the refrain of a traditional gospel song.

4. This quotation is from the refrain of "O I Want to See Him" (1916), lyrics by R. H. Cornelius.

· CHAPTER 10 ·

# The Steps of a Good Man

## Eulogy for Stephen James

MARY H. YOUNG
PSALM 37:23-24

*The steps of a good man are ordered by the LORD: and he delighteth in his way. Though he fall, he shall not be utterly cast down: for the LORD upholdeth him with his hand.* (Psalm 37:23-24 KJV)

The sermon, crafted in the expository form, was written and preached by Mary H. Young. Mary is assistant professor of Christian education and director of the Master of Arts in Christian Education program at the Samuel DeWitt Proctor School of Theology at Virginia Union University and senior minister at the St. John United Holy Church in Richmond, Virginia. This sermon is a great example of how intimate knowledge of the deceased can provide the basic building blocks for the sermon. With great pastoral sensitivity, Mary builds the introduction of the sermon from shared experiences of the deceased's personality and work in the community of faith where he was a member and where she had previously served as Interim Minister. With this, she grabs hearers' attention, prepares the congregation to explore a straightforward exegesis of Psalm 37, and establishes the theme of the eulogy: the deceased was a good man.

Each of the two points which follow are drawn directly from exegesis of the psalm, and one side of each point or move in the sermon is devoted to how that exegesis correlates to the life of the deceased and the community of faith. Throughout, Mary weaves together the life experiences, struggles, and contributions of the deceased and the "assurance of grace" found in the words of the psalm. This sermon also demonstrates a clear pastoral theology of death and dying as Mary, in the celebration of the sermon, lifts the congregation to resurrection hope as a consequence of God ordering the steps of a good man.

We have gathered today to say farewell to a good man—Deacon Stephen James. With heavy hearts warmed only by our memories of his life, his person, his wit, his love, his devotion to his wife, his fellowship with friends and family, and his incredible commitment to the Lord, today we wipe away tears mingled with smiles. Stephen had suffered for a number of years with his health, but if the truth be known, his zest for life never made him seem ill. He made the best of every day and lived life to the fullest. So . . . we were not ready for this moment, even though Stephen James had made all of his necessary preparation. His body has now betrayed him, but even on this day, we feel his contagious spirit in this place. On this day . . . we have delightful memories of Stephen that are embracing and comforting us—making us laugh and cry all at the same time. He was a good man.

I'm sure that all of you have your Stephen James stories, just as I have mine. I have quite a few. But as I reflected, Sister Melva, on what I would say here today, there was one passage of Scripture that commended itself to me as an appropriate salute to Stephen. It is these two verses found in this well-known and familiar psalm. We may know verses of this psalm by heart. Listen to the part that describes Stephen: "The steps of a good man are ordered by the Lord: and he delighteth in his way. Though he fall, he shall not be utterly cast down: for the Lord upholdeth him with his hand."

Stephen James was a compassionate, frank, direct, to-the-point, genuine, lively, and humorous man. He was a matter-of-fact guy who told you like it was even if you didn't like it. If you didn't want to hear the truth, then don't ask him. Because he wasn't going to beat around the bush; he was going to tell it like it was. He was a good man!

This passage of Scripture provides a powerful portrait of Stephen. There is a contrast in Psalm 37 between the wicked and the righteous. The psalmist informs us that those who love the Lord find favor in God's sight. In fact, not only does God guide the life of God's own, but also God delights in, or is pleased with, the way that they live and the service that they give. God directs the affections, thoughts, and actions of good people. By God's providence, God overrules the events that concern them, so as to make their way plain. God goes before them to guide them step by step. God protects them in the time of trouble and embraces them through the turbulence of life. The Lord knows the ways of the righteous, and with favor orders their every step. God takes delight in the way of the righteous. "The steps of a good man are ordered by the LORD: and he delighteth in his way."

Stephen James was a good man! God knew him, and he knew God! A whole lot of people might know you by name and be familiar with your walk. They might even bear testimony to your steps . . . but does God know you? Can the God of the universe, the omnipotent, omniscient, and omnipresent Creator, take delight in your way? God knew Stephen James—but so did many of us. My last conversation with my friend took place the Monday prior to his death. He called me that Monday morning, and we talked for a long time about various and sundry things, but his main reason for calling was to alert me that he would be going into the hospital for a procedure toward the end of that week. His voice sounded strong, happy, and content. His call reminded me of a promise he asked of me some months ago. It became fresh again. Stephen James had looked me in the eye and made me promise him that I would do his eulogy. Though he was asking me to be polite, I knew that I really didn't have a choice in the matter. And of course, I said yes. I was afraid not to. So on Monday, as we talked, I remembered my promise. As we ended our conversation I said something to him that I had never really expressed before—though I hope that he already knew it! I said, "Stephen James . . . I love you, my brother!" And he replied back to me, "I love you too, Doc!" And with that, we ended our call. I was left with a mysterious feeling that it would be our last time talking—though it was too painful for me to allow it to linger in my spirit. Not only did God know this good man—I knew him too! "The steps of a good man are ordered by the LORD."

Our church family has lost a good man, whose way we knew well and whose steps were evident in our midst.

We saw his steps as a faithful and committed deacon.

We saw his steps as a mentor to young men of the church.

We saw his steps as a man of integrity and strength.

We saw his steps as a van driver, member of the male chorus, diaconal disciple, family ministry team leader, regular attendee at Sunday school and Bible study, friend and confidant.

We saw his steps as a committed member who was often here when the doors opened and the last one to leave after the doors were closed.

I experienced his steps as on Wednesday evenings after Bible study he would not leave until I was in my car. And if he was unable to stay, he would order Deacon Belvin Simmons to get the job done. He was a good man!

"The steps of a good man are ordered by the LORD: and [the LORD] delighteth in his way."

The next verse of that psalm (v. 24) adds even greater specificity to this favored position that Deacon Stephen James had with God. It reads, "Though he fall, he shall not be utterly cast down, for the LORD upholdeth him with his hand." Sister Melva, I know that Stephen was special to you, but you know what? He was also somebody special in God's eyesight. Contrary to our thinking of this fall as a falling into sin, the psalmist means something totally different. What he really means is that though the righteous one falls into sickness, though the righteous one falls under the power of adversaries, though the righteous one falls into distress, though the righteous one falls into trials and tribulations, though the righteous one falls into despairing circumstances, he shall not be utterly cast down . . . because the Lord upholds him with his hand! It may appear that right is on the scaffold and wrong is on the throne, but there is a God standing in the midst . . . keeping watch over God's own. God upholds him with his hand!

Brother Stephen had his share of trouble, difficulty, and health challenges. As his health began to fail, he felt the strain of living life with discomfort and pain and the frustration of not being able to do and go as he pleased.

He wanted to drive, and there were times when he didn't feel up to it.

He wanted to rest lying flat in his bed, but there were times when it was more comfortable to sit up.

He wanted to work, but his doctors forbade his involvement in strenuous activities.

He wanted to maintain his regular schedule of activities, but his body would often betray him.

Yet in the midst of it all—this good man could claim the precious assurance that suffer though he may, he would never be utterly cast down. For the Lord upheld him with his hand.

Deacon Stephen James knew trouble, but he also knew where his help came from. He must have embraced the words of the apostle Paul, who raised the question, "Who shall separate us from the love of Christ? Shall tribulation, or distress, or persecution, or famine or nakedness or peril or sword? As it is written, For thy sake, we are killed all the day long; we are accounted as sheep for the slaughter. Nay, in all these things, we are more than conquerors through him that loved us. For I am persuaded, that neither death, nor life, nor angels, nor principalities, nor things present, nor things to come, nor height, nor depth, nor any other creature, shall be able to separate us from the love of God, which is in Christ Jesus our Lord."[1]

The Lord upheld Stephen James with his hand!

## Celebration:

Sorrow may bring us to the earth, and death may bring us to the grave, but when our steps are ordered by the Lord, we will rise again, because the Lord upholds us with his hand. Brother Stephen knew where his help came from. On one day during the last week of his life, Melva said she heard him in the bedroom praying for her and asking God to give her strength because he knew that she would have a hard time upon his leaving. The steps of a good man are ordered by the Lord! On another day during that last week of his life Deacon Stephen James made his way down to the riverbank where he loved to relax and fish. I believe that he and the Lord had a good talk. As he sat there, he called Deacon Allison to tell her just how peaceful it was . . . down by the river. He was talking about an earthly place that day, but even then, it had special spiritual significance.

At that river, the burdens of his soul rolled away.
At that river, angels came and ministered unto him.
At the river, he could hear the insect chorus singing the glorious praises of God.
At the river, Brother Stephen could feel his soul connecting with his Savior.

Sister Melva, peace was beckoning him—at that river.
Grace was giving him strength for the days ahead.
And God was assuring him that it was all right to come on over on the other side.
No more dialysis.
No more heart procedures.
No more medicine.
No more discomfort and restlessness.
No more fatigue and slowness of steps.
Where the wicked shall cease from troubling and the weary shall be at rest.
Where every day will be Sunday, and the Sabbath will have no end.
Where God shall wipe all tears from his eyes.

---

**NOTES**

1. Romans 8:35-39 KJV.

· CHAPTER 11 ·

# An Unusual Response

## Eulogy for Martin Garnett

CLAUDE R. ALEXANDER JR.
2 SAMUEL 12:15-25

*But when David saw that his servants whispered, David perceived that the child was dead: therefore David said unto his servants, Is the child dead? And they said, He is dead. Then David arose from the earth, and washed, and anointed himself, and changed his apparel, and came into the house of the Lord, and worshipped: then he came to his own house; and when he required, they set bread before him, and he did eat. Then said his servants unto him, What thing is this that thou hast done? thou didst fast and weep for the child, while it was alive; but when the child was dead, thou didst rise and eat bread. And he said, While the child was yet alive, I fasted and wept: for I said, Who can tell whether God will be gracious to me, that the child may live? But now he is dead, wherefore should I fast? can I bring him back again? I shall go to him, but he shall not return to me.* (2 Samuel 12:19-23)

This expository eulogy is written by Claude R. Alexander Jr., the senior pastor of the Park Church (formerly the University Park Baptist Church) in Charlotte, North Carolina; president of the Hampton University Ministers' Conference (2011–2014); and bishop in the Kingdom Association of Covenant Pastors, led by Dr. Walter Scott Thomas.

In this eulogy, Claude does what he describes as a twofold or threefold exegesis. Teasing deeper biblical meanings from the text, he sensitively exegetes the life of the deceased while exploring the complex issues raised by the untimely death of a young child. While embracing the parents' necessary journey through sorrow, Claude turns the family and congregation back toward worship and faith. He reminds the parents and other mourners that the child's departure foreshadows every human's destiny; we all will meet again in eternity.

Finally, in the celebration, Claude draws the congregation into what must have been a rousing assurance that no difficult life event ultimately thwarts God's purpose. He concludes the celebration with a restatement, an almost catechetical roll call of biblical quotations signaling the fulfillment of God's loving and redemptive purpose in Christ.

MILTON AND SHARRELL, WE COME to be with you in this celebration of Martin's life and of your ministry as parents. We sit with you as you grieve his loss. We commend you for your lives as mother and father. We admire your faith, your courage, and your determination. We've been inspired by your defiance. We've been touched by his smile and by his fight. For reasons only known to God, Martin's earthly race was short, yet his experience of your love and support was sweet.

Very few have sat exactly in your seat. Very few can imagine that walk that has been yours and the walk that is now yours. However, there is One who knows completely. That is God. God is sufficient for you in this hour and for the hours, days, months, weeks, and years ahead.

When thinking about a word to declare to you, I was led to the story of one who experienced your experience. His name is David. We know him as the man after God's own heart and the anointed of the Lord. Like you, he experienced the sickness and death of a child at a young age. The circumstances surrounding the sickness and death are very different from yours; however, the experience of fear, anxiety, loss, and grief are very much the same.

With verse 16, we find that David pleaded with God day and night for the child's healing. He fasted. He refused to eat, or even bathe. On the seventh day, the child died. The servants were reluctant to tell David out of fear of what he might do. They were afraid that he might harm himself. Upon seeing the servants whispering, David inquired about the status of the child. The servants told him that the child had indeed died. Verse 20 provides David's response.

David arose, bathed, anointed himself, put on some clean clothes, went to the house of the Lord, worshipped, and then went home and ate a meal.

This totally blew the minds of the servants. To be honest, it blows my mind as well. During the child's illness, David didn't sleep, eat, bathe, or worship. All that he did was plead for the child's life. Upon the child's death, he bathes, worships, and eats. How could he act like this? Is he in denial? Has he had a psychotic break? What is going on?

The servants, out of curiosity, ask David about it. David responds, "While the child was alive, I fasted and wept; for I said, 'Who can tell whether the LORD will be gracious to me that the child may live?' But now he is dead; why should I fast? Can I bring him back again? I shall go to him, but he shall not return to me."[1]

When I looked at this, I wanted to let David talk to you. This is what David said: "Milton and Sharrell, I know that kind of pain. I felt it. I lived it. And you may be wondering how, upon my child's death, I could get up and get back to life. You may wonder about the possibility of getting up and getting back to life. I want to let you know how I did it."

## 1. Worship Is Natural to a Believer

"When I heard about my child's illness, I prayed. I called on the Lord in supplication. I pleaded with the Lord. I maintained a connection with the Lord. I fasted. I let the Lord know how serious I was about the matter. However, with all of that, the outcome was what it was. With that, there was a battle in the spirit. What would be my position with God? After spending days and nights pleading and fasting before God, how would I be toward God when I didn't get what I pleaded and fasted for?

"There were two ways that I could have responded. I could have responded by distancing myself from the Lord. Or I could draw even closer to the Lord. For most of my life, I've been a worshipper. I'm known for the psalms that I sing unto the Lord. I'm the one who provides some of the great psalms of the faith: Psalm 23, Psalm 27, Psalm 34, Psalm 4, Psalm 18, Psalm 51. Worship has been second nature to me. Worship was all that I had when I was on the run. In fact, sometimes, the only thing that I had was my worship. Therefore, I resorted to the one thing that I know works—worship. I put myself into the presence and the worship of God. I needed to be in the presence of God, and I needed my expressions to be Godward. There's something calming and comforting about the presence of the Lord. I needed to reaffirm the goodness of God, the faithfulness of God, the love of God, and the presence of God in my life.

"The believer in the Lord has the privilege of knowing God and of getting into the presence of God. The believer has the blessing of being able to let the presence of God be a shield, be a refuge, and a healing balm. The believer has the awesome opportunity of rehearsing the person and power of God through worship and finding strength in being reminded about the person of God. Worship becomes a part of your arsenal. In this time, you need to be put in remembrance that God is still God. God is still sovereign. God is still in control. God is still present. God is still good. God is still faithful. God is still with you. God is still on your side. The Lord is still your light and salvation."

## 2. God Enlarged My Understanding of Grace

"The content of my pleading was that God would be gracious and let the child live. I tied the graciousness of God to the survival of my child. I equated the grace of God to God extending the life of my child. However, my child died. Some would say that with the death of my child, God was not gracious.

"As I sat there, I was led to understand that even with my child dying, God had been gracious to me. The truth of the matter is that I should have died. The death should have been mine. However, God made a promise that an eternal line would come through me. That line had yet to be established. God's promise to me and God's purpose for me kept me alive even when it didn't keep the child connected to me alive. Yes, I lost my child, but God extended God's grace toward me and kept me alive.

"It may be difficult to affirm right now, but you are evidence of the grace of God. No, Martin is no longer with you, but you still have each other. You are alive. God has kept you. In the midst of the darkest experience of your life, God has kept you. Every day, you've awakened. Every day you've existed and survived. This should extend your understanding and gratitude. As God's grace has sustained you, God's grace will sustain you. God's grace will keep you. God's grace will be sufficient for you.

"I could bathe, worship, and eat, not simply because worship was natural to me and God enlarged my understanding of grace, but also because I know something about eternity."

## 3. I Know Something about Eternity

"My faith in God provides me with a unique perspective about eternity. My child entered into eternity. My child entered into the presence of God. Wish all that I might, I can't bring the child back to me. However, I will go to him. I'm not here to stay. I too have a date with eternity. There is but a step between me and death. There will be a time when I will go where my child has gone. I'm not uncertain about it. I'm not unsure about it. I'm not hazy about it. I know where I'm going. I put it in one of my psalms. I sang it."

> Yea, though I walk through the valley of the shadow of death, I will fear no evil: for thou art with me; thy rod and thy staff they comfort me. Thou preparest a table before me in the presence of mine enemies: thou anointest my head with oil; my cup runneth over. Surely goodness and mercy shall follow me all the days of my life: and I shall dwell in the house of the LORD for ever.[2]

Like David, every believer in the Lord should know something about eternity. This world is not our home. There is another land. There is another place. It's Job declaring, "I know that my redeemer liveth, and that he shall stand at the latter day upon the earth."[3]

Because of his knowledge of Jesus Christ, Paul could write, "For we know that if our earthly house of this tabernacle were dissolved, we have a building of God, an house not made with hands, eternal in the heavens."[4] Through our Lord and Savior Jesus Christ, we have the promise of resurrection and reunion. Jesus declared, "I am the resurrection, and the life: he that believeth in me, though he were dead, yet shall he live: and whosoever liveth and believeth in me shall never die."[5] Jesus assured us, "Let not your heart be troubled: ye believe in God, believe also in me. In my Father's house are many mansions: If it were not so, I would have told you. I go to prepare a place for you. And if I go and prepare a place for you, I will come again and receive you unto myself; that where I am, there ye may be also."[6]

Jesus died that we might have life eternal. Because of Jesus, we have the hope of reunion. "Therefore, we do not grieve as others who have no hope."[7] "For if we believe that Jesus died and rose again, even so them also which sleep in Jesus will God bring with him."[8] "We which are alive and remain unto the coming of the Lord shall not prevent them which are asleep. For the Lord himself shall descend from heaven with a shout, with the voice of the archangel, and with the trump of God: and the dead in Christ shall rise first: then we which are alive and remain shall be caught up together with them in the clouds, to meet the Lord in the air: and so shall we ever be with the Lord."[9]

David says, "I have a date with my child because I have a date with the Lord God. I could get up and get back to my life through worship that was second nature, an expanded understanding of God's grace, and a perspective concerning eternity. But there was another thing."

## 4. God's Promise and Purpose Were Still Alive

"The death of my child did not signify the death of God's promise and purpose. God still had a promise over me and a purpose within me. I had to press toward the promise and the purpose. God had kept every word that God promised. God kept God's word of correction. God's word had promised an heir. I had to move on knowing that God had a word to keep.

"Milton and Sharrell, you have to press through the tears, the pain, the questions, toward the promise and the purpose of God. Every day, God will give you strength to press through and to press toward. In pressing through and in pressing toward, God produced a son. God gave me a son whose name was Solomon. There was another name given to him. It's the name Jedidiah, which means 'God's beloved.' God let me know how much he loved me. God will let you know how much he loves you. God will present and provide manifestations of his love and grace."

"When you know that the Lord loves you, you can make it. Life may be rough, but you know that the Lord loves you."

When it gets difficult to affirm the love of God because of circumstances, all that you need do is remember the word, "Herein is love, not that we loved God but that God loved us and sent his Son to die for us."[10] "For God so loved the world, that he gave his only begotten Son, that whosoever believeth in him should not perish, but have everlasting life."[11] "But God commendeth his love toward us, in that, while we were yet sinners, Christ died for us."[12] How do you know that God loves you? Look yonder on a hill called Calvary, and see Jesus dying for the sins of us all. Know that there is nothing that shall separate you from the love of God in Christ Jesus![13]

**NOTES**

1. 2 Samuel 12:22-23 NKJV.
2. Psalm 23:4-6 KJV.
3. Job 18:25 KJV.
4. 2 Corinthians 5:1 KJV.
5. John 11:25-26 KJV.
6. John 14:1-3 KJV.
7. 1 Thessalonians 4:13 NRSV, paraphrased.
8. 1 Thessalonians 4:14 KJV.
9. 1 Thessalonians 4:15-17 KJV.
10. 1 John 4:10, paraphrased.
11. John 3:16 KJV.
12. Romans 5:8 KJV.
13. Romans 8:39.

▪ CHAPTER 12 ▪

# Beautiful Feet

## A Eulogy for Rev. Barry T. Young

PETER M. WHERRY

ISAIAH 52:1-7

Awake, awake,
put on your strength, O Zion!
Put on your beautiful garments,
O Jerusalem, the holy city;
for the uncircumcised and the unclean
shall enter you no more.
Shake yourself from the dust, rise up,
O captive Jerusalem;
loose the bonds from your neck,
O captive daughter Zion! . . .
Therefore my people shall know my name; therefore in that day they shall know that it is I who speak; here am I.
How beautiful upon the mountains
are the feet of the messenger who
announces peace,
who brings good news,
who announces salvation,
who says to Zion, "Your God reigns." (Isaiah 52:1-2, 6-7 NRSV)

The sermon that follows was written for the funeral of my best friend, Rev. Barry T. Young.[1] Although this sermon is a full manuscript and not simply an outline, in deference to the occasion (a worship service attended by persons and speakers from all over the country), it is written in a somewhat abbreviated style. It is designed to portray the deceased, in various roles of his life, as the long-awaited messenger who comes bearing good news of Israel's emancipation from captivity. It was also designed to show Barry, through his faithful life in Christ, emancipating us, the mourners, from the captivity of our grief.

In his treatise on *Friendship and Old Age*, Marcus Tullius Cicero said, "Comradeship has within it all that men most desire." Barry Young was my dearest friend. There are three of us best friends: Barry, Micah, and Peter, "the three musketeers." Mary, Jackie, and Wanda are our beautiful, powerful, and gifted wives. In fact, there are three couples of us, friends. We have been like brothers and sisters for the better part of thirty years. Barry and Mary Young have been our friends since before we were married. In June, Wanda and I celebrated twenty-seven years of marriage. The wedding of Mary and Barry was the first social occasion Wanda and I ever attended as husband and wife. We were married in June, and they were married that same summer in August. We have celebrated the births of our children, we have watched them grow, we have spent holidays together, we have laughed and cried, we have said farewell to loved ones—all together. The fellas even have a tradition of going to King's Dominion without the ladies. This last trip, we made a pact not to divulge to the ladies how we've gradually decreased the number of rides we got on as the years have gone by. Today is the first time we have had to bid farewell to anyone in our precious little circle.

In addition to the pain, Barry's departure has caused some intense reflection on the meaning of each of our lives and on the meaning of one another. As the years have passed and I watched him walk the various roads of his life, I began to understand more completely just how special and how truly excellent Barry T. Young was. He was a first-rate scholar. It was Barry who convinced me that the two of us needed to go to Wesley Seminary to get doctor of ministry degrees. Together we drove back and forth to Washington, him driving, and because of his driving, me praying! Together we sat through class after class, and I watched with admiration his absolute brilliance. He made me proud to be from Virginia Union, as those from Harvard and Drew and Princeton and other places struggled to keep up with us. He shared his parents with me while we were in DC, and the Youngs opened their home and treated me like their own son.

He was a phenomenal father, not just to his beloved Jessica but to Makeda (Micah and Jackie's daughter) and Bethany and Justin (our children), too. The "three musketeers" became even closer when our daughters were born. We each watched over our children like hawks, and when it came to our daughters, we had a tradition of getting together and (with some tongue in cheek) examining prospective boyfriends who would come to call, or sometimes we'd carefully interrogate our daughters about what was under these young men's fingernails. Barry doted on his beautiful Jessi like our loving God, carefully shaping the first human soul. He went into her room when she was a baby every night, laid his hands on her, and prayed through grateful tears. Almost every picture of Jessica has Barry in it. He took his baby out to dinner as a rite of passage when she began to become an incredible young woman, and he modeled for her the epitome of what a real man should be. He set the standard; only intense, sacrificial, vigilant, forthright, and faithful love can be real love.

He was a superlative husband. Mary was the queen of his life, and he was her adoring and absolute admirer. I loved to hear him talk about how beautiful she is. Barry was naturally outspoken, but if you ever wanted to quickly see his bad side, just let him think you caused Mary Young any heartache. Mary and Barry were joined together in their souls. They have spent the last twenty-seven years becoming one flesh.

Barry was a biblical son. As great a leader as he was, around his parents, it was moving to see his intentional deference to a noble father who brought the Bible to the dinner table, and a mother who loved him with passion and relentless support. He looked after his parents. When either of them was ill, he went to the rescue. He interrogated doctors like Johnny Cochran.

Barry was a wonderful brother. He could have fun with the best of them, full of teasing and jokes, and once he started laughing, the whole room got tickled. His mischievous grin was infectious. He had a way of letting you know that you could tell him anything, and that whatever trust you reposed in him was well-placed.

Barry was an exemplary pastor. I have always said that if there ever was a pastor I wanted to be like when I "grow up," it was

Barry. He loved Mosby.[2] If you were his member, you could be sure that a shepherd was watching over your soul. He loved every person, even those who acted as his enemies. He loved the young and the seniors and everyone in between. He was the most loving pastor I have ever known. He would give and give and give, many times going when he didn't have energy left to go. He was a good steward, carefully protecting the resources and good name of the church. He lived without complaint in the fishbowl of ministry. He was a preacher par excellence. No spiritual junk food was ever served at Barry Young's hands. He was a faithful and diligent exegete. When he picked up the hem of his robe while preaching, you knew he was about to "huff and puff 'till he blew the house down!"

Etched forever in my memory is Barry's fifteenth and final pastoral anniversary at Mosby this past July. The Youth Praise Dancers of Mosby presented a moving routine to the song by Donald Laurence entitled "Beautiful Feet." The words to the song are based upon the text from Isaiah 52:7: "How beautiful upon the mountains are the feet of the messenger who announces peace, who brings good news, who announces salvation, who says to Zion, Your God reigns."

It may be that the most impressive aspect of Barry Young's life was the journey he took toward death. True to form, he understood implicitly that no person's journey is traveled only for himself. Barry was careful to interpret for all of us the meaning of this last journey because he knew how difficult it would be for us to travel. When we knew that Barry's time of departure was near, he came home, and some of his beloved sisters-in-law had arrived as he was being brought back to the house. After we got him settled, I was privileged to sit down in the living room next to one of Mary's powerful sisters, Rev. Annie Smith. She informed me that on one of their many previous visits, Barry called all of Mary's sisters who were there around the bedside and gave them this message: He wanted them to encircle and support Mary because he now had to walk two roads. One road he described as a road of faith. He needed to believe that the God he served was able to miraculously heal his body. The other road he described as a road of acceptance. He needed to be able to accept that this same God may not choose to heal him in this life.

When I heard this profound poise and power modeled by my friend, I also heard, while sitting in the living room, this text. As

Barry walked the roads of life as friend, as scholar, as father, as husband, as brother, as son, as pastor, he has been for us all a messenger with beautiful feet. Especially as a man walking these last, the dual roads of faith and acceptance, he has shown up again on the horizon, and lest any of us who are grief-stricken by his recent journey misunderstand, even in this he has beautiful feet.

After a long sojourn in the dark valley of Babylonian captivity, the prophet calls for Israel to wake up, get up, and shake off the dust of slavery's sleep. The nation is challenged to look up to the mountains to witness a life-altering phenomenon. The sentinels, who are trained and accustomed to peering into the predawn mist on the lookout for enemies, are now exhorted that a new day has broken. This is no message of doom. This is indeed a message of deliverance. The long night of oppression has ended, and the morning of Yeshu'ah, of salvation, has dawned. Elohim has come in the person of this messenger to declare that that which is sown in corruption has, in fact, put on incorruption.[3] So the messenger with the beautiful feet declares to those of us gathered today in Good Shepherd Church:[4]

> Listen! Your sentinels lift up their voices,
>     together they sing for joy;
> for in plain sight they see
>     the return of the LORD to Zion.
> Break forth together into singing,
>     you ruins of Jerusalem;
> for the LORD has comforted his people,
>     he has redeemed Jerusalem.
> The LORD has bared his holy arm
>     before the eyes of all the nations;
> and all the ends of the earth shall see
>     the salvation of our God.
>
> Depart, depart, go out from there!
>     Touch no unclean thing;
> go out from the midst of it, purify yourselves,
>     you who carry the vessels of the LORD.
> For you shall not go out in haste,
>     and you shall not go in flight;

for the LORD will go before you,
    and the God of Israel will be your rear guard.

—Isaiah 52:8-12 (NRSV)

Even now, I can hear the man with the beautiful feet say,

Just as soon as my feet strike Zion,
I'm gonna lay down my heavy burden;
Put on my robe in glory,
Shout and tell the story

Over the hills and mountains,
Come to the Crystal Fountain.
All of you sons and daughters,
Come to the healing waters.
I shall wear a golden crown![5]

**NOTES**

1. This is another of only a few instances throughout this book in which the names of the deceased, his family, and others are utilized. This decision was made because the family is a prominent one and already well-known nationally. I have also obtained permission from Barry's widow, Rev. Dr. Mary H. Young, to utilize the eulogy as presented.

2. The Mosby Memorial Baptist Church is where Barry served as pastor for fifteen years.

3. See 1 Corinthians 15:42.

4. While Barry was pastor at Mosby Memorial, that church sanctuary was not large enough to accommodate the huge crowd who attended his homegoing service. Thus, the funeral was held in Good Shepherd Baptist Church of Richmond, Virginia, where Dr. Sylvester Smith served as pastor.

5. This is an excerpt from a gospel song which has been sung among African Americans for nearly a hundred years. The lyrics are in the public domain; the song is known by least two titles: "I Shall Wear a Crown" and "Just as Soon as My Feet Strike Zion."

· CHAPTER 13 ·

# Acceptance, Praise, and Thanksgiving

## A Eulogy for Royzell Dillard

DEBRA HAGGINS

JEREMIAH 29:11

*For surely I know the plans I have for you, says the* LORD, *plans for your welfare and not for harm, to give you a future with hope.* (Jeremiah 29:11 NRSV)

This eulogy, written by Debra Haggins, is also in the inductive style. This sermon, however, is markedly different from that in the preceding chapter in terms of context. The first was preached at a funeral service in a church sanctuary. This was preached by a university pastor on a college campus, and the context was a memorial service, not a funeral. The occasion was the sudden and unexpected death of a longtime and greatly beloved university choral director, Royzell Dillard.[1] Debra does a unique and creative job of crafting a conversation about the thorny issues of death and loss, based upon the chosen text, between the deceased and God.

AS A CHILD, I WAS TAUGHT to never question God. In my home, even the hint of questioning God was too close to a lapse in faith. Questioning God was too close to incomplete trust in the sovereign power of an all-wise, all-present, all-powerful, everywhere-at-the-same-time, never-early/never-late/on-time God.

There was no questioning the God of our salvation. Logic did not apply, the scientific method was inappropriate and not compatible, and philosophical thinking was faulty. So I was bred such that even if you forgot your name, address, and Social Security number, you had better remember that God is holy, sovereign, never makes a mistake, and owes me no explanation. This is what you do when you don't understand the will and the works of God: accept it, praise God through it, and then thank God for it. When life hurts, when the unexplainable, when the unacceptable, when the intolerable, when the unbelievable, when the painful and the sorrowful intrude on our lives, the advice is to accept God's will and God's work, praise God through it, and then thank God for it.

Yes, preacher, you are right; that is easier said than done. It was difficult to do last Thursday night around 11:00 p.m. We found it difficult to accept that Mr. Dillard had gone home to be with the Lord. It was difficult to praise our way through the tears and the questions through the disbelief and the shock. But I found it a little easier and a little more comforting to thank God for the life that was Royzell's. To thank God for this gifted man who crossed our paths. So rather than cross the line and participate in any semblance of questioning our God, I have chosen to imagine this conversation between Mr. Dillard and the Lord. I have chosen to honor God and pay tribute to Mr. Dillard with the imagining of a divine dialogue between the Creator and the creation.

I am honored first of all to give this eulogy, fortunate to have been a colleague, and pleased that he called me his pastor. It was in Clarke Hall where I learned of his extreme love for all things musical, especially his students and choirs. But gone now are the days of auditions, rehearsals, tours, and concerts.

Now, as the news of Mr. Dillard's passing began to give way to reflections and ponderings, I imagined a divine conversation between God and Mr. Dillard much like the conversations God had with the prophet Jeremiah. Please allow me to honor Mr. Dillard in this special way.

I imagined that the Lord spoke to Mr. Dillard in the fiftieth year of his life as they had spoken many times before. I imagined the Lord saying to Mr. Dillard, "Royzell, as it shall be with all of humankind, it is now time for you to come and be with me and the angelic hosts in heaven." However, Mr. Dillard responded and said, "I hear you, Lord, yet I have so much to do. There are concerts to book and tours to plan. I am gearing up for the annual Thanksgiving concert and benefit; I'm readying myself for *Messiah* in anticipation of honoring the birth of your Son and my Savior, Jesus Christ. There are rehearsals and auditions; there is the spring break tour and the Choir and Organists' Guild. Lord, there are voices and musicians to nurture and conducting students to train." And the Lord simply said, "It is time, Royzell."

"Lord, you have placed so much in me, invested so much in me, gifted me and afforded me opportunity after opportunity, bestowed upon me both blessings and privileges. I can't leave the work just yet; there is still so much to be done. Why stop me now?"

And I could hear God saying, "Royzell, do you believe that I am sovereign?"

"Yes, Lord!"

"Royzell, do you believe that your life has always been in my hands?"

"Yes, Lord!"

"Royzell, do you love me?"

"Yes, Lord, you know I do."

"Then know this: there is a bigger plan at work here. My plan, son, is greater than death. I chose you when you were a baby back in Memphis. In fact, I chose you before you were formed in the womb of your mother. I chose you. I called you. I gifted and anointed you. I, your heavenly Father, chose you to be a light in a dark world, and boy, did you shine! I placed you over hundreds or thousands of students during the past twenty-five years so that my plan for your life—your destiny—could be fulfilled and the earth made richer because you were here.

"You see, Royzell, even in death, I still know the plans I have for you, plans to give you a hope and a future. You looked for me, and you found me. You searched for me with all of your heart, and you found me.

"Son, it is not the length of your years that matter, but the magnitude of your life's influence that makes the difference. Hundreds of students, thousands of lives changed, made richer and better because of you. Your work on earth is complete, Royzell. It is finished!"

"My friends, my colleagues, my students who are like family to me, what will they say? How will they feel?"

"They will miss you, and they will hurt for a while because of what you meant to them and what you've invested in them. Your students past and present will always remember you. You will always be the remembered as a gifted inspiration, motivation, and benchmark of excellence."

"And finally, God, what do you say about me?"

"That's easy, son, I was there in the beginning, and I am right here (right here with you) in the end. What do I say about you, you ask? I say, 'Well done, my son, well done!'"

And with sweet peace and an absolute resolve, Mr. Dillard flashed that trademark smile and handed the baton over to the master Conductor and said, "Nevertheless, Father, not my will but your will be done. It is well, oh so well, with my soul."[2]

## Conclusion

And even now as we are grieving, please know that it is well with Mr. Dillard. Every single one of us in this room is on assignment from God. We have all been sent to be light in a dark world. And when the assignment is over, God calls his ambassador home. Music was his gift; music was his life. Mr. Dillard used his gift and his life to light the world. His assignment was to change the world one note at a time. A symphony does not begin as a fully composed work, but a symphony begins with just one note. A choir does not begin with a completely rehearsed song, but they sing to the glory of God with the first, single note. If we are going to get through the missing of Mr. Dillard, we are going to have to do it one note at a time.

Royzell's journey is complete! Royzell's assignment is over! Now God has called his ambassador home!

But what about you? Will you be ready when God calls you home? Have you made Jesus Christ the Lord of your life? Do you have a relationship with Christ? If you have never said yes to your assignment, if you have never said yes to your ambassadorship, if you have never said yes to salvation, if you have never said yes to God's free gift of eternal life, today is your day!

Because, you see, everybody has to start from somewhere. This is a celebration of Mr. Dillard's life, but I also hope that it brings you to this resolve: I don't know when death is coming. I don't know the circumstances. I don't know the situation. I don't know whether I will be surrounded by friends or whether it will find me alone. All I know is that with whatever time I have left, I'm going to stay the course. I am going to finish the race. I'm going to embrace every challenge with whatever time I have left, and the clock is ticking on everybody. I might not like what I'm feeling right now; I don't feel like celebrating. I don't have the strength to celebrate, but the one thing I have left is more than a celebration. What I've got left is the sacrifice of praise and thanksgiving! And so I'll praise God, because Royzell passed our way!

I'll praise God because the battle has been fought, the victory is won![3] Let's praise God because there in glory is a crown, that pearl of great price,[4] and we wouldn't take nothing for our journey right now![5]

---

**NOTES**

1. Because of the public nature of his death, the actual name of the deceased is utilized in the manuscript.

2. For Jesus; words in Gethsemane ("not my will . . ."), see Matthew 26:39, 42; Mark 14:36; Luke 22:42. "It is well" paraphrases slightly a line from the refrain of the hymn "It Is Well with My Soul" (1873), with lyrics by Horatio G. Spafford (1828–1888) and music by Philip P. Bliss (1838–1876). This hymn is in the public domain.

3. This is a slight paraphrase of a line from the hymn "Servant of God, Well Done!" (1819), with lyrics by James Montgomery (1771–1854) and music (1852) by Isaac B. Woodbury (1819–1858). This hymn is in the public domain.

4. Matthew 13:46.

5. Maya Angelou, *Wouldn't Take Nothing for My Journey Now* (New York: Random House, 1993).

• CHAPTER 14 •

# The Nine Lives of Cat Moss

## A Eulogy for My Mother

GREGORY K. MOSS SR.
PSALM 90:10

Our days may come to seventy years,
    or eighty, if our strength endures;
Yet the best of them are but trouble and sorrow,
    for they quickly pass, and we fly away. (Psalm 90:10 NIV)

This eulogy, the third and final one in the inductive style, was written by Gregory K. Moss, Sr. Greg is the senior pastor of the St. Paul Baptist Church of Charlotte, North Carolina, and is the president of the Lott Carey Baptist Foreign Mission Convention. He is the immediate past-president of the General Baptist State Convention of North Carolina. He was recently inducted into the Morehouse Board of Preachers. With remarkable word economy, Greg uses a verse from Psalm 90 to tell the story of the life, struggle, and death of his mother, Catherine Moss.[1] The deceased's dying request was for her son, Greg, to preach her eulogy. (Interestingly, this sermon never was preached. At the time of Cat Moss's death, Greg's son was so grief-stricken that he needed his dad in the pew during the service. Now, for the first time, this wonderful sermon will get a hearing.) The life, struggle, and death of Greg's mom creates a parallel of sorts to kerygma (the life, death, and resurrection of Jesus). While this sermon does tell the poignant story of the life of Greg's mom, it also grounds the listener squarely inside the love, grace, and care of God, who finally, through death, raises the suffering mother to a new life. This sermon is very much a story. It is indirect speech at its best (see chapter 5).

IN PSALM 90, THE ONLY ONE attributed to Moses, emphasis is placed upon the brevity of life. It follows a thread found in Job: those born of woman are of few days and those are full of trouble, trials, tribulation, struggle, and strife.[2] Writing with a hand honed by the experience and wisdom of old age, Moses further stressed our brevity is often soured by suffering and sadness. Life has a rhythm. There are highs and lows, ins and outs, ups and downs. And at certain times, this life is marked by limitations and toil, as the text enlightens.

This word is befitting of the rhythm that was the life of my mother. Like many, Mom was no stranger to the challenges that accompany this journey. She loved and lived her life with great zeal. She loved her family, enjoyed her friends, never met a stranger, and squeezed every ounce out of life and then some from what was available to her. Equipped with dry wit and a love for laughter, she was often the life of the party. And she loved a good party!

Through the years I have listened to colleagues attribute their success as pastors to the faith and strength of parents who are or were pillars of the church. Not so in our household. Mom was not a particularly religious person. She did not occupy a particular pew on Sunday. She was not a frequent attendee of regular major celebration days. She would never be mistaken for the mother of the church. She was never present to cast a vote during a juicy church confrontation—I mean conference. In fact, I never heard her quote long, uninterrupted passages of Scripture or pray fervent, soul-stirring public prayers. But my mother was a good, wholesome person, instilling within me "stuff": drive and values she believed a man should possess.

Over the years, our relationship as mother and son ebbed and flowed. Eventually we experienced a role reversal. I became totally responsible for her well-being. However, she was still Mom and had no problems reminding me and the world of that fact. Formally she was known as Catherine Moss. I called her Mom, but to close friends and family she was affectionately known as Cat Moss. And I believed she was appropriately labeled Cat.

There is a widely held myth that cats have nine lives. Cats by nature are finicky, feisty, and agile, possessing tremendous leaping ability. It is believed they always land on their feet. I have observed cats leap from unbelievable heights, landing on their feet. I too have playfully tossed cats into the air to see if they landed on their feet, and almost always they did. The myth evolved from the practice of some ancient cultures that tossed cats from towers, expecting them to land on their feet. Often they did; sometimes they did not. Though injured, they survived and would rise and run away.

Cat Moss, not unlike her feline namesake, was metaphorically tossed from the towers of life. Tossed by ailments that hampered or claimed the lives of many, fueling my belief she too had nine lives. At the age of thirty-five, Mom had a kidney removed and never went on dialysis. She developed and lived with rheumatoid arthritis in both hands. She developed and lived with emphysema. She suffered through multiple mini-strokes. She struggled with double pneumonia four times. She suffered three heart attacks. She developed dysplasia on her uterus. She was diagnosed with cervical cancer. And finally, Mom was beset with lung cancer that spread to her spine, leading to her ultimate appointment with God.

Cat Moss was one tough lady. With all her ailments, one could not gaze upon her and see the evidence of disease. Like her clothes, she wore her challenges well and maintained class, dignity, and elegance even while preparing to die. Perhaps you too can celebrate with me on this blessed day that Cat Moss surely had at least nine lives.

I am eternally grateful for her love and undying loyalty and support. In this, she never wavered. Though she may not have been the perfect picture of a strong, religious matriarch in the eyes of some, she made tremendous contributions to the kingdom. I understand that now. Mom made me go to church. No matter what, I was required to ride that church bus or jump in the back seat of Deacon Bob Hill's Caddy and go to Sunday school and stay for worship. Rain or shine, sleet or snow, she made me go. "How unfair is that?" I recall thinking to myself, living by the mantra "Do as I say do, not as you see me do." But I understand now. In her own way, Mom's spirituality was being exercised vicariously through me. By some spiritual osmosis, she experienced God by positioning the gift he had given her to be exposed to his Word, will, and way. She believed I would become somebody of value and virtue and one day do good and prosper.

Thank you, Mom, for all you did for us. And because of you, your sacrifices, and your wisdom, I can mount this sacred desk and with confidence say a word on your behalf, reminding the people of the quiet greatness God instilled in you. Yes, you were appropriately labeled Cat. "Threescore years and ten," the Bible says, "and if by reason of strength they be fourscore years, yet is their strength labour and sorrow."[3] For seventy-six years, you were tossed from the towers of this life by ailments beyond your control. And like your namesake, each time you either landed on your feet or rose from your side and went your way to live your life. However, on the cool, quiet evening of March 13, God decided you'd had enough of being tossed from the towers of this life. You landed on your feet, rose from your side, assuaged your wounds, purring and extending your life. But you achieved something your namesake could not: you were given another life, an extension of life, an ailment-free life, a medicine-free life, a pain-free life, a toss-free life; eternal life. You, my dear mother, have your own myth and will forever be remembered in my mind as the Cat with ten lives! To God be the glory. We love you.

**NOTES**

1. In this eulogy, actual names are used with the permission of the preacher as the deceased's surviving son.
2. See Job 14:1.
3. Psalm 90:10 KJV.

# Epilogue

*To the extent that the word-perception of the gospel of hope has grasped us, to that extent we can believe in the goodness and power of God and with thanksgiving accept the future he gives.*[1]

PREACHING IS A PRIVILEGE. There has never been a preacher since Jesus who merited the honor of heralding the Good News. It is vital, therefore, that all of us who approach the task do so with the same mindset as good theologians: tentatively. Every preacher sees some light concerning the awesome task of preaching, but not one of us is the lighthouse. We all do the best we know how, and sometimes we manage to do the best we can. None of this is absolution from a duty of diligence and living as a lifelong learner.

It is my prayer that if this volume has done nothing else, it has opened up some new ways of thinking concerning the preaching task and provided some fresh approaches to using the tools of homiletics, especially during a time of bereavement. I pray that every preacher during a time of bereavement understands that much work on the sermon must be done within the social location of the family prior to the day of the funeral, and even prior to the writing of the sermon. It is my hope that every preacher who reads this text will be humble enough to learn from each aspect of the grieving process and from every encounter with grieving people.

The journey toward healing is a spiritual and homiletic laboratory within which astute expositors will rightly learn the art and science of preaching. No preacher worth the ink on his or her ministerial license will attempt to handle human hearts during a time of death without first formulating a sophisticated, personal, and intelligible theology of death and dying. This theology must be grounded in the Christian Scriptures and shaped by the preacher's existential encounters with death. A preacher's theology concerning death must also be animated by a personal faith in the God of the Bible, including the Sovereign over death, who is Jesus Christ, and the Holy Spirit, who is the catalyst for both faith and praxis.

It was my intention to provide in these pages concise guidance for both identifying and selecting a text for preaching, so that the content of preaching can be more potent and meaningful to listeners and so that the journey toward healing can begin. It has finally been my intention to add value to the ways in which preachers approach the task of constructing the sermon, so that the preaching/sermonic trumpet may be sure to give a more certain sound. No sermon should be hijacked by confusion or disorder, because when hearts are broken by death, listeners need to know that God has a plan and that there is a "Bright Side Somewhere."[2]

This is the task of funeral preaching: to bring perspective to pain. When all is said and done, no one grieving or even seeking salvation on a Sunday morning will be the least bit interested as to whether there is a word from the preacher. In their times of uncertainty and grief, what will bring perspective to their pain is an affirmative answer to the question, "Is there any word from the Lord?" (Jeremiah 37:17 NIV).

**NOTES**

1. Milton Crum Jr., *Manual on Preaching: A New Process of Sermon Development* (Wilton, CT: Morehouse-Barlow, 1988), 159.

2. This is the title of a gospel song, the date of which is unknown. Its music and lyrics were written by "Blind" Reverend Gary Davis (1896–1972), a native of Laurens, South Carolina. This song has been rerecorded by numerous gospel artists over the years, and many of them never gave proper credit to its composer. Reverend Davis is a little-known legend of blues and folk gospel music that has influenced scores of blues and rock instrumentalists, among them Bonnie Raitt, The Grateful Dead, Bob Dylan, and Jackson Browne. Additional information on Reverend Gary Davis can be found at http://new.music.yahoo.com/reverend-gary-davis/biography/ (accessed February 17, 2011).

# About the Contributors

**Claude Richard Alexander Jr.**, DMin, is the senior pastor of The Park Church in Charlotte, North Carolina, as well as the current president of the Hampton University Ministers' Conference. He also serves on the boards of *Christianity Today* and Gordon-Conwell Theological Seminary.

**Brad R. Braxton** is Lois Craddock Perkins Professor of Homiletics at Southern Methodist University in Dallas, Texas. He is also the founding senior pastor of The Open Church in Baltimore, Maryland. He holds a PhD in New Testament studies from Emory University and an MPhil in theology from the University of Oxford, where he was a Rhodes Scholar. His ordination is with the National Baptist Convention, USA.

**Nathan Dell**, MDiv, is seminary homiletics instructor at the Samuel DeWitt Proctor School of Theology at Virginia Union University, Richmond, Virginia. He is pastor emeritus at the Woodville Presbyterian Church in Richmond, where he served for thirty-two years (1964–1996).

**Debra L. Haggins**, MDiv, was licensed by the American Baptist Churches USA, and ordained as a Progressive Baptist minister. Rev. Haggins serves as chaplain of Hampton University and is executive director and treasurer of the Hampton University Ministers' Conference. She is also the pastor of the University's Memorial Church, an interdenominational campus chapel.

**Toney L. McNair Jr.**, DMin, was ordained by the American Baptist Churches, USA and the Historic Queen Street Baptist Church of

Norfolk, Virginia. Dr. McNair serves as the associate pastor for worship at the historic First Baptist Church of Norfolk, Virginia. He also teaches Choral Music and is Department Chair of the Fine Arts Achievers Academy, grades 6–8, for the Indian River Middle School (Chesapeake, Virginia). Dr. McNair serves as the Vice President of the Chesapeake Education Association VEA/NEA and is a board member and Admin/Finance Chair with the Chesapeake Community Services Board. He is the author of *Let's Have Church: A Guide for Worship in the African American Context* (rev. 2011).

**Gregory K. Moss Sr.**, DMin, is the senior pastor of the St. Paul Baptist Church of Charlotte, North Carolina. He also serves as president of the Lott Carey Baptist Foreign Missions Convention, a global missions agency of Baptist heritage.

**Mary H. Young**, EdD, is assistant professor of Christian education and director of the Master of Arts in Christian Education program at the Samuel DeWitt Proctor School of Theology at Virginia Union University. Dr. Young also serves as minister at the St. John's United Holy Church in Richmond, Virginia.